GAY
CINEMATHERAPY

Also by Beverly West

Culinarytherapy: The Girl's Guide to Food for Every Mood

Also by Beverly West with Nancy Peske

Cinematherapy for the Soul: The Girl's Guide to Finding Inspiration One Movie at a Time

Cinematherapy for Lovers: The Girl's Guide to Finding True Love One Movie at a Time

Advanced Cinematherapy: The Girl's Guide to Finding Happiness One Movie at a Time

Bibliotherapy: The Girl's Guide to Books for Every Phase of Our Lives

Cinematherapy: The Girl's Guide to Movies for Every Mood

Frankly Scarlett, I Do Give a Damn! Classic Romances Retold

GAY CINEMATHERAPY

The Queer Guy's Guide to Finding Your Rainbow One Movie at a Time

By Jason Bergund and Beverly West

UNIVERSE

First published in the United States of America in 2004
by UNIVERSE PUBLISHING
A Division of Rizzoli International Publications, Inc.
300 Park Avenue South
New York, NY 10010
www.rizzoliusa.com

© 2003 by Jason Bergund and Beverly West

2004 2005 2006 2007/ 10 9 8 7 6 5 4 3 2 1

Printed in the United States of America

ISBN: 0-7893-1054-6

Library of Congress Catalog Control Number: 2004104604

Illustrations © 2003 by Maurice Vellekoop

Designed by Headcase Design
www.headcasedesign.com

To best friends everywhere,
who defy gravity and build bridges to
the future, just by being themselves.

Acknowledgments

We would like to thank our editor Kathleen Jayes for her impeccable taste and guidance. Thanks also to our agent Neeti Madan for her optimism and encouragement, and to Pam Sommers for her hard work and enthusiasm. A very special thanks to Maurice Vellekoop for his inspired and insightful illustrations, and to our friends and family, who are the pot of gold at the end of our rainbow.

JASON: I would like to thank all of my couchmates for making girls' nights so much more fun, especially LJ and Jen Edwards, Rich Haslow, Lori Wiley, Arnie Mejia, Nancy Peske, Kristen Kreft, Gretchen Krull, Josh and Amy Kent, Karin Dorell, Shabnam Shakibaie, George Martino, and Diana DeCola. A special thanks to my co-author, co-dog owner, and my partner in crime and life, Bev West; you brighten each and every day of my life.

BEV: Thanks to the gay men in my life, especially Sean McKenna, John Giuliano, Mark Wisnewski, Richie Fusco, LJ Edwards, and Rich Haslow, who have all been a bridge over troubled water, and taught me that when the going gets tough, the tough throw a theme party. Thanks also to Nancy Peske, Kim Doi, Ron Hayden, Ellen Rees, Joe Kolker, Tom Pennacchini, Pam and Lily Eisermann, and my parents Marilyn and Bill Knox for their love and confidence. A very special thanks to my partner Jason Bergund, my unexpected happily ever after, and a brave and constant companion on the road less traveled by.

CONTENTS

INTRODUCTION

Finally, a video guide that understands what gay men have known for years . . . the Oscars aren't just an awards show but the Gay Super Bowl, and movies are more than entertainment . . . they're best friends and a form of therapy that can help us cope with everything from a coming-out crisis to the home-alone-homo blues.

Gay Cinematherapy prescribes the right remote-control remedy to help you find the comfort, inspiration, humor, and inner-beauty tips that you need, without looking any farther than your neighborhood video store.

Got a bad case of boogie fever but can't manage a trip over the rainbow this weekend? Plug in with a Vicarious Party Pic, and dance the night away without ever getting up off your couch. Closet getting a little short on air that doesn't smell like mothballs? Take a deep breath with a Coming-Out-of-the-Closet movie and be reassured that as long as there is love in your heart, you'll never walk alone. Feeling maudlin and full of self-pity? Satisfy the urge to purge with a Drama-Queen movie and enjoy the crime without doing the time.

Drawing on gay-themed and mainstream movies from the past and present, and with an extra helping of anything starring Judy, Bette, Bette, Joan, and Madonna, we focus on heroes and heroines that speak directly to the gay soul and remind us that the true measure of a man is not the size of his bus, but whether he can pull off a crinoline strapless and a pair of platform pumps and still get out of the desert alive.

We've also included inspirational quotes we'd like to see printed on a pride banner; Jason's Barmacy, with cocktails designed to wet your inner whistle; Bev's Hideaway and Laundrette, offering self-pampering rituals that are like fabric softeners for the soul; and "Don't Do It," featuring movies with homophobic or disempowering messages that aren't really gay friendly at all.

So whether it's a bad breakup, a "no more wire hangers" moment, or the urge to embrace your inner drag queen, *Gay Cinematherapy* offers the cinematic road map you'll need to help you find your rainbow, one movie at a time.

Questions? Comments? Movie suggestions? Write to us at gaycinematherapy@aol.com.

CHAPTER ONE

DON'T LET THE DOOR HIT YA

WHERE THE GOOD LORD SPLIT YA:

Coming-Out-of-the-Closet Movies

Come on, now. Be honest. You took up tap dancing by the time you were twelve. By sixteen you were making Barbra Streisand mixes for your friends' moms, and making memories at band camp. And currently you're planning a catered affair in anticipation of Liza's next comeback. So how much longer are you going to keep insisting that you're one thing, when you feel so much like the other?

Coming out is something that we all have to do at least once in our lives, and more than likely, it's something we'll do at various points along life's highway, as we venture out into new territories.

Coming out is about a lot more than admitting to the world that you're in the market for something a little different than a girl just like the girl who married dear old dad. Coming out is a process of accepting who you are, standing up for what you believe in, asserting your right to be happy, and demanding that people finally accept some difficult truths—like real men really do drink mimosas and love the Golden Girls.

So if your emotional closet is getting a little short on fresh air, tear down that bitch of a bearing wall and put a window where a window ought to be. Then pop in one of these Coming-Out-of-the-Closet movies about heroes who have found the courage to be who they are, or learned the high cost of denying the truth, and let the sun shine out.

C A M P (2003)

STARS . . . . Anna Kendrick, Daniel Letterle, Chris Spain,
. . . . Don Dixon, Sasha Allen, Tiffany Taylor, Joanna Chilcoat

DIRECTOR . . . . Todd Graff

WRITER . . . . Todd Graff

If you're having trouble finding your role in the musical comedy of life, let the kids at *Camp* remind you that sometimes fitting in means finding the courage to stand out.

Michael, Dee, Vlad, Ellen, Jill, and Jenna are all aspiring actors on their way to "Camp Ovations" for a summer of song, dance, and denial. Michael, who wore a dress to his prom, is a pimple-faced gay teenager trying to unwind his tangled life. His new roommate, Vlad, is an OCD straight guy who uses music to cope with the pressures of his rocky adolescence. Ellen, Jill, and Jenna all think that the measure of a woman is her dress size. Through ballads and breakdowns, costumes and choreography, friendships and fights, and, of course, plenty of good old-fashioned musical theater, this talented group of friends discovers that getting a standing ovation on the stage of life means knowing who you are, loving who you are, and not being afraid to sing it loud and sing it proud.

THE PRINCIPLES OF FLIGHT

"Come to the edge, he said. Come to the edge,
though you may fall. Come to the edge, he said. And they came.
And he pushed them. And they flew."
GUILLAUME APOLLINAIRE

"Kites rise highest against the wind, not with it."
WINSTON CHURCHILL

DON'T ASK, DON'T TELL:
QUESTIONS WE REALLY DON'T WANT ANSWERED

"Have you ever experimented with heterosexuality?"

DANIEL LETTERLE

AS VLAD IN *CAMP*

"When I was eight years old I told my dad that I wanted to take an acting class. He said, 'There are fifty billion people in this world, if one-tenth of 1 percent of them wanted to be actors, that would still be five million people. Do you really think you're prettier than five million people? You're not even the prettiest girl in your class.'"

JOANNA CHILCOAT

AS ELLEN IN *CAMP*

Tommy: "Do you accept Jesus Christ as your personal savior?"

Hedwig: "No, but I love his work."

MICHAEL PITT AND JOHN CAMERON MITCHELL

AS TOMMY AND HEDWIG IN *HEDWIG AND THE ANGRY INCH*

"So you feel your mother betrayed you?"

BARBRA STREISAND

AS SUSAN LOWENSTEIN IN *THE PRINCE OF TIDES*

BEAUTIFUL THING (1996)

STARS .... Glen Berry, Scott Neal, Linda Henry, Tameka Empson

DIRECTOR .... Hettie MacDonald

WRITER .... Jonathan Harvey, based on the play by Jonathan Harvey

If you've been turning a deaf ear to the song in your heart because you're afraid your tune is a little off-key, let Jamie's (Glen Berry) and Ste's (Scott Neal) beautiful thing remind you that if you want to make your own kind of music, then you've got to sing your own special song, whether or not anybody else sings along.

Set in a tenement in the East End of London (read British trailer park), Jamie, a round peg in the square hole of high school, cuts class just to avoid football, and pines for Ste, the popular and athletic boy next door, literally. When Ste moves in with Jamie's family to avoid his father's and brother's abuse, a love grows between these two new immigrants from the island of misfit toys, who begin to find love, acceptance, and harmony in each other.

Surrounding these two innocent, vulnerable, and yes, totally adorable young lovers, are a whole host of characters who are each, in their own ways, struggling to come out about something. There's Jamie's mom, Sandra (Linda Henry), who is trying to free herself from her bad taste in men; Leah (Tameka Empson), the iconoclast next door who's trying really hard to come out about something although we're not quite sure what; and then, of course, Ste and Jamie themselves, who discover that when you find the courage to sing your unique melody solo, you'll inspire those around you to join in and harmonize.

H U L K (2003)

STARS..............................Eric Bana, Nick Nolte, Jennifer Connelly

DIRECTOR..Ang Lee

WRITERS...........................James Schamus, story by James Schamus,
..............................based on characters by Stan Lee and Jack Kirby

Unbeknownst to himself, Bruce Banner, an arrogant and aloof regeneration scientist and the son of a brilliant but controversial genetic engineer, is not your average chip off the old block. He is, in fact, the product of his father David's narcissistic attempts to mold his own DNA into that of a super-soldier capable of defending the world against foreign invasions. Uh-huh.

What David (Nick Nolte) doesn't realize, however, is that his bent DNA is unwittingly passed on to his son and lies dormant just waiting for an excuse to erupt.

One day, while innocently experimenting with gamma-activated nanomeds in his laboratory, Bruce is accidentally exposed to radiation. Instead of killing him, however, the radiation makes him stronger. In an instant, his hidden hulkhood, a kiwi-hued metaphor for repressed rage and unaddressed sexuality, is unleashed.

From this day forward, whenever Bruce gets stressed out, these powers and appetites that he never asked for, and which have by now been blown way out of proportion through years of expertly engineered repression, emerge and create havoc for poor Bruce, who usually has a lot of explaining to do the next morning.

It is only when Bruce embraces his inner hulk that he is able to control the beast within and become the heroic super-soldier that nature intended him to be.

So if your inner primate is rattling the bars, but you're afraid to let the gorilla out of the cage, let the Hulk remind you that sometimes the thing we're most afraid of inside ourselves is the very thing that gives us strength, and that the beast within may not be a beast at all, but a hero just waiting to strike a blow for truth, freedom, and the American way.

JASON'S BARMACY

TRUTH SERUM

Growing up, much like breaking up, is hard to do. And there are times when you need to zip your lip, inhabit your space, and think things through. But then there are times when you need to cut loose with that old gang of yours and let the good times roll. When that happens, be sure to serve a little "Truth Serum" on the rocks and celebrate the beauty of self-discovery, together.

You will need:

• 2 ¼ ounces of orange or citrus vodka

• ¼ ounce of Rose's lime juice

Here's how you do it:

Put everything in a shaker with lots of ice and shake, shake, shake. Serve in a cute highball on the rocks. Garnish with a thin lemon slice.

INTERVIEW WITH THE VAMPIRE (1994)

STARS . . . . Tom Cruise, Brad Pitt, Kirsten Dunst, Antonio Banderas

DIRECTOR . . . . Neil Jordan

WRITER . . . . Anne Rice, based on the novel by Anne Rice

Okay, so a story about two Gothic allegories with over-developed incisors who haunt the back streets of antebellum New Orleans in search of human prey may not seem like the most obvious choice when you're looking for the courage to come out of the closet. But Anne Rice's metaphorical, not to mention preternaturally gorgeous, fiends provide a great lesson about the living death that results when we deny ourselves the nourishment that we require to truly live.

Louis (Brad Pitt), a promising young plantation owner with golden curls, a golden future, and an uncanny ability to pull off a pair of knickers and a ruffled tunic and still look masculine, is consumed with a gnawing discontent after the death of his wife in childbirth. Louis's pervasive grief threatens to transform his fertile and expansive acreage into a murky bayou of unrealized potential.

Unrealized, that is, until Louis gets cruised by the vampire Lestat (Tom Cruise), and after one too many rum hurricanes in a leather bar on the wrong side of town, he lets Lestat teach him a thing or two about the meaning of surrender. Lestat plucks Louis from the gangplank of denial and depression, tears off the blindfold, and lifts Louis up the full length of a very large and very Freudian mast pole, and then releases him with a great splash into the midnight waters of forbidden pleasure. From that moment forward Louis is transformed, and resist though he may, he is compelled to return again and again to sample Lestat's heady, wet indulgences. Arm in arm they hunt the parkways and boulevards on the right side of town, decked out in tastefully coordinated ensembles complete with top hats and bedazzled canes, searching for fresh blood in the elegant salons of the southland before they drove old Dixie down. Yet even in the midst of this banquet of four-star vampire cuisine, Louis is so plagued by guilt that he can't enjoy his supper, which doesn't make him a very popular dinner companion. And so eternity for Louis becomes just like one long, dateless, not to mention hungry, Saturday night when nobody calls and the cable is out.

So if you're feeling hungry in the shadows and frightened by your own irrepressible appetites, let Louis's struggle for self-acceptance remind you that the only road to peace, love, and satisfaction starts with appreciating ourselves for who we are.

QUOTES FROM THE CRYPT

"Merciful death! How you love your precious guilt."

. . . .

"You are a vampire who never knew what life was until it ran out in a big gush over your lips."

TOM CRUISE
AS LESTAT IN *INTERVIEW WITH THE VAMPIRE*

"The statue seemed to move, but didn't. The world had changed, yet stayed the same. I was a newborn vampire weeping at the beauty of the night."

BRAD PITT
AS LOUIS IN *INTERVIEW WITH THE VAMPIRE*

"They had forgotten the first lesson—that we are to be powerful, beautiful, and without regret."

ANTONIO BANDERAS
AS ARMAND IN *INTERVIEW WITH THE VAMPIRE*

FAR FROM HEAVEN (2002)

STARS.......Julianne Moore, Dennis Quaid, Dennis Haysbert, Patricia Clarkson

DIRECTOR...Todd Haynes

WRITER...Todd Haynes

This stylized vision of the fifties ideal, dissecting the life of a picture-perfect husband and wife who are anything but what they seem, reminds us all that no matter how high the cost of admitting our true feelings, it's always a better bargain than trying to buy a lie.

Julianne Moore stars as Cathy, a June Cleaver-esque housewife—only with a better wardrobe designer—who is the apotheosis of ideal fifties housewifery. On the surface, Cathy appears to have it all. She has the perfect house, perfect pumps to match her perfect lipstick, perfect kids, and the perfect husband (Dennis Quaid). Or is he?

When Frank starts developing a few pesky habits, like getting cranky around the house, drinking too much at neighborhood parties, and sleeping with random men, Cathy must come to terms with the fact that there may be a few things she doesn't know about her husband.

So what's the apotheosis of ideal fifties housewifery to do? Why, begin a taboo affair with an African-American gardener, of course, and sow a few wild oats of her own. She reaps more than she sows, however, when she falls in love with the gardener and discovers first-hand how difficult it is to admit to a forbidden passion in an unforgiving society, and harder still to live without your true heart's desire.

If you've been afraid to let your hair down for fear you'll shock the neighbors, watch *Far from Heaven* and let this love letter from a more restrictive past remind you that if you want to get to heaven, you've got to raise a little hell.

JULIANNE'S JAWBREAKERS

"We ladies are never what we appear,
and every girl has her secrets."

JULIANNE MOORE

AS CATHY WHITAKER IN *FAR FROM HEAVEN*

"I am trying to have a complete nervous breakdown,
and no one will let me do it in peace!"

JULIANNE MOORE

AS ALICE GOODWIN IN *A MAP OF THE WORLD*

"I've worked around predators since I was twenty years old.
Lions, jackals, hyenas . . . you."

JULIANNE MOORE

AS DR. SARAH HARDING IN *JURASSIC PARK*

"No, how could I? I'm just a humorless ice queen
in desperate need of a good humping."

JULIANNE MOORE

AS DR. ALLISON REED IN *EVOLUTION*

FOOTLIGHT FANTASIES: BECAUSE SOMETIMES YOU'VE JUST GOT TO INDULGE YOUR INNER SHOW-TUNE QUEEN

A CHORUS LINE (1985)

STARS......................Michael Douglas, Terrence Mann, Vicki Frederick,
....Alyson Reed, Cameron English

DIRECTOR..Richard Attenborough

WRITERS......................Arnold Schulman, based on the stage musical
........................with book by Nicholas Dante and James Kirkwood Jr.,
.........................music by Marvin Hamlisch, lyrics by Edward Kleban

Who hasn't dreamed of putting on those gold sequin outfits, standing in that famous line, and strutting his or her stuff? For many, the stage is one of the few places that feels like home.

When Zach (Michael Douglas) opens up the stage door for auditions, everyone in New York City with tap shoes is lined up to land a spot on the line. After cuts are made and tears are shed, we're left with a dozen talented hopefuls. Things take an interesting turn when it's not talent Zach is looking for, but personality. Everyone on the stage is forced to come out if he or she wants to land this job.

So when you're feeling the need to come out and be a part of the chorus, take your spot on the line and celebrate your own inner singular sensation.

THE PHYSICS OF THE CLOSET

"Doors don't slam open."
JOHN M. SHANAHAN

**"I'm sort of a gay success story, a very inspirational one.
What happened to me is exactly the opposite of what
closeted people fear: They think they'll lose everything
if they come out. This did not happen to me at all.
In fact, everything came back tenfold."**
MELISSA ETHERIDGE

**"I just wish more of my fellow queers would
come out sometimes. It's nice out here, you know?"**
ELTON JOHN

**"It's no wonder we know how to dress:
We've spent centuries in closets."**
ISAAC MIZRAHI

**"It takes courage to grow up and turn out
to be who you really are."**
E.E. CUMMINGS

SUGAR SHACK
THE MAN-CANDY COUNTER

KEANU REEVES

BE (Bedroom Eyes), **SIN** (Smoldering, Inscrutable, Noble), **LGIL** (Looks Great in Leather), **CHE** (Come-Hither Eyewear)

TOP TESTOSTERONE PICS: *Speed, My Own Private Idaho, The Matrix, The Matrix Reloaded, The Gift, Devil's Advocate, The Watcher*

ERIC CHRISTIAN OLSEN

RTAA (Really Tempting Adam's Apple), **TADAARBNDT** (That Adorable Dumb-as-a-Rock, Boy-Next-Door Thang), **SGG** (Sexy Gap-toothed Grin), **LGIPB** (Looks Great in Puca Beads)

TOP TESTOSTERONE PICS: *Dumb and Dumberer: When Harry Met Lloyd, Local Boys, Mean People Suck, Pearl Harbor*

ERIC BANA

LCWHA (Looks Cute When He's Angry), **RUM** (Raw, Unpredictable Masculinity), **SEMA** (Sexy Early Man Appeal), **LGIG** (Looks Great in Green)

TOP TESTOSTERONE PICS: *The Hulk, Black Hawk Down*

BRAD PITT

RGH (Really Great Hair), **EPA** (Eight-Pack Abs), **EOTDBOY** (Emblematic of the Doomed Beauty of Youth), **GITCGS** (Gorgeous in the Classic Greek Sense)

TOP TESTOSTERONE PICS: *Thelma and Louise, Legends of the Fall, Oceans Eleven, Fight Club, A River Runs Through It, Interview with the Vampire*

TOM CRUISE

SIN (Smoldering, Inscrutable, Noble), **GAGFOS** (Grows a Great Five O'Clock Shadow), **PBE** (Piercing Blue Eyes), **TSLGT** (That Sexy Little-Guy Thang)

TOP TESTOSTERONE PICS: *Risky Business, Mission Impossible, Top Gun, Days of Thunder, Rain Man, Cocktail*

DJIMON HOUNSOU

LGOAC (Looks Great on a Catwalk), **SIN** (Smoldering, Inscrutable, Noble), **TAAAA** (Totally Amazing Abs and Arms), **CHE** (Come-Hither Eyewear)

TOP TESTOSTERONE PICS: *Lara Croft Tomb Raider: The Cradle of Life, Biker Boyz, Heroes, Gladiator*

ANGELINA JOLIE

BLLIH (Best Lower Lip in Hollywood), **RGC** (Really Good Cheekbones), **VPUB** (Very Provocative Utility Belt), **TSDAEBST** (That Sexy, Digitized, and Extremely Busty Superhero Thang), **LGIACS** (Looks Great in a Chase Scene), **SIN** (Smoldering, Inscrutable, Noble), **HTBGOA** (Has the Biggest Gun of All)

TOP TESTOSTERONE PICS: *Gia, Girl Interrupted, Pushing Tin, Lara Croft: Tomb Raider, Lara Croft Tomb Raider: The Cradle of Life, Original Sin*

EDGE OF SEVENTEEN (1998)

STARS . . . . Chris Stafford, Tina Holmes, Andersen Gabrych, Lea DeLaria

DIRECTOR . . . . David Moreton

WRITER . . . . Todd Stephens

So you're not a boy, not yet a man, and you've got one foot in the closet and one foot on a banana peel. Join forces with Eric (Chris Stafford), break down the door, and come out with both feet planted firmly on the ground of adult self-acceptance.

Stuck in retro Ohio the summer before college, Eric starts his job at a nearby theme park but winds up riding more than the roller coaster. As is often the case at theme parks, it's not long before gay co-worker Rod, yes, Rod (Andersen Gabrych), penetrates Eric's defenses, and they hit the sheets—after which Eric slams his closet door again, this time making sure he locks it behind him. Emphasis on the word *behind*.

Overwhelmed and confused, Eric turns to best girlfriend Maggie (Tina Holmes) for support. With Maggie's unconditional love, his own increasing confidence, and a little attention from Rod to back him up, Eric finally comes out of the closet with bells on. Well, more like a Chris Issak hairdo and lots of eyeliner, but you get the idea. With the support of lesbian boss Angie (Lea DeLaria), Eric breaks the news to Mom and Dad; they are less than pleased but ultimately learn to accept the truth about their son.

So when the winds of change start rattling your shutters, put on your ripped jeans and remember when—because if you made it past the edge of seventeen, you can make it through anything.

 REALITY CHECK

Your humble co-author, Jason, spent his edge of seventeen at the very same Ohio theme park as Eric. Only Jason appeared in a lavaliere that went all the way down to his waist.

GAY CINEMATHERAPY

BEU'S HIDEAWAY AND LAUNDRETTE

FABRIC SOFTENERS FOR THE SOUL

If life has been rubbing you the wrong way lately and you're beginning to feel a little chapped, battle the elements with this fruit facial guaranteed to leave you feeling refreshed and ripe for the picking.

You will need:

- 1 ripe and juicy tomato, chopped
- 1 teaspoon lemon juice
- 1 tablespoon instant oatmeal

Here's how you do it:

Throw all of your ingredients into a bowl and stir until you form a gloopy mess that's thick enough to cling to those problem areas. If the mixture isn't thick enough, add more oatmeal. Then slather the whole mess onto your face and relax for twenty minutes, for God's sake. Then wipe the whole mess off with a warm moist cloth.

AUDIOTHERAPY

"I AM WHAT I AM" ANTHEMS

When it's time to kick open the closet and crank up the music, there's nothing better than these "I am what I am" anthems to help you celebrate yourself at full volume.

"I'M COMING OUT"
DIANA ROSS

"HERE'S WHERE I STAND"
CAMP SOUNDTRACK

"BEAUTIFUL"
CHRISTINA AGUILERA

"I WILL SURVIVE"
GLORIA GAYNOR

"WE ARE FAMILY"
SISTER SLEDGE

CHAPTER TWO

WHEN YOU'RE MAUDLIN

AND FULL OF SELF-PITY

Drama-Queen Movies

It happened again, didn't it . . . just like you said it would. But does anyone listen to you? Oh, no! Of course not. No one ever pays any attention to you. God forbid anyone should consider good old trustworthy, reliable, rational, not to mention unselfish, you. Why should anyone treat you with the same common courtesy and respect that they would show to any stranger on the street? He'll understand one day. He'll see the error of his ways, he'll be sorry, and if he's not, you'll make him sorry. But until that day of reckoning comes, bring the curtain down with one of these Drama-Queen movies that will satisfy the urge to purge, encourage you to leave the drama on the screen where it belongs, and get back on the path toward musical comedy.

THE HOURS (2003)

STARS . . . . Nicole Kidman, Julianne Moore, Meryl Streep, Ed Harris

DIRECTOR . . . . Stephen Daldry

WRITERS . . . . David Hare (screenplay),
. . . . based on the book by Michael Cunningham III

If you're in the mood for a little overkill, paint the town blue with this cinematic triple scoop of rocky road, featuring three world-class drama queens, all with a whopping case of the icks, who reassure us that one good pout really can ruin everybody's party for the better part of a century—and beyond.

In 1924, Virginia Woolf (Nicole Kidman in that nose) writes the novel *Mrs. Dalloway*, while wading deeper and deeper into the pregnant waters of narcissism and depression and making everybody around her feel really, really guilty about it.

In 1951, Laura Brown (Julianne Moore) reads the novel *Mrs. Dalloway*, while wading deeper and deeper into the pregnant waters of narcissism and depression and making everybody around her, feel really, really guilty about it.

In 2001, Clarissa Vaughn (Meryl Streep) becomes Mrs. Dalloway, submerging her entire existence into a vain attempt to cheer up her best friend Richard (Ed Harris), an AIDS-afflicted, mother-fixated poet who is wading deeper and deeper into the pregnant waters of, you guessed it . . . narcissism and depression, and making everybody else, particularly Clarissa, feel really, really guilty about it.

So if you're in the mood to get down and roll in it, let this tri-generational saga of death and rebirth guide you into the delicious downstream of despair, and then set you back safely on shore, where you can dry off and enjoy the picnic with a renewed appetite for life.

TRUTH OR DARE (1991)

STARS . . . . Madonna, Madonna, Madonna, Madonna (and Warren Beatty)

DIRECTOR . . . . Alex Keshishian

The undisputed doyenne of the drama (besides, maybe, Michael Jackson) invites a hand-held camera on her "Blonde Ambition" tour and gives us all a backstage look at what life is really like for a world-class drama queen. Along the way, Madonna teaches us that when the going gets tough, the tough fire their road managers, hire people who won't make so many goddamn mistakes, and book a world tour.

The Material Girl hits the road with a gaggle of gay dancers, two backup singers who can really sing, one hair and makeup person, two daddy issues, one cynical yet adolescent movie-star boyfriend, sixty-three wigs, four lavalieres, and one big, bad attitude.

The whole thing is one long Madonna buffet. We see Madonna facing down William Morris agents, faulty monitors, and the horrified Canadian authorities. We see Madonna and company dressed, undressed, and wearing those weird cone-shaped bra thingies that would have given Otto Tittsling a cramp. And then there are the drinking games after hours at the hotel, Dolce & Gabbana, and Warren Beatty getting really, really disgusted by the whole damn thing. But mostly we see Madonna . . . Madonna high, Madonna low, and every Madonna in between, at the point in her life when nobody but nobody could tell her no.

So if you've been having a little trouble exerting creative control in your life, watch *Truth or Dare* and take a few tips from the mistress of manipulation, who doesn't settle for second-best and isn't afraid to put love to the test. The next time you're ready to pitch a diva-sized hissy fit, take a moment and let Madonna remind you to be sure that you're the one signing the paychecks, honey; because otherwise, you might find yourself playing to an empty house.

MADONNA'S MOCHACCINOS

"We shouldn't have any more sex. You should build an altar for me
in your home and worship it daily, and call me collect!"

MADONNA

AS HERSELF IN *TRUTH OR DARE*

"I can't believe you came all the way out here without
a fucking cell phone!"

MADONNA

AS AMBER IN *SWEPT AWAY*

"I'm gracing this armpit of a town for one night. If you think
I'm gonna know the name of the VENUE in El Arm-Pitto . . .
you're sadly mistaken."

MADONNA

AS STAR IN *THE HIRE: STAR*

"Hi, my name's Mae, and that's more than a name—that's an attitude."

MADONNA

AS "ALL-THE-WAY" MAE MORDABITO IN *A LEAGUE OF THEIR OWN*

"I know how you feel. You don't know if you want to
hit me or kiss me. I get a lot of that."

MADONNA

AS BREATHLESS MAHONEY IN *DICK TRACY*

ALL ABOUT EVE (1950)

STARS..............................Bette Davis, Anne Baxter, George Sanders,
....Celeste Holm, Marilyn Monroe

DIRECTOR...Joseph L. Mankiewicz

WRITER...Joseph L. Mankiewicz

Look, girl, we know how it is, okay? One minute you're the toast of Broadway with a devoted and passionate young director on your arm, fawning reviewers, a personal playwright, a full-time hair and makeup person, and one staff member whose only job is to carry your hoopskirt to the laundry. The next thing you know, you're slamming headfirst into forty, your young and passionate director sells out to Hollywood, your playwright falls in love with your understudy, and suddenly the signature fire and music of your creative peak has turned into a tin kazoo and a couple of sparklers. The worst part is, nobody, not even your best friend, seems to give a damn.

So what's an aging but legitimate grand dame of the stage to do when her star begins to sputter? Why, watch a Bette Davis movie, of course, and learn from the best how to relieve a little of your own stress by inflicting it on everyone around you.

Bette Davis stars as Margot Channing, a first-class doyenne of the drama whose midlife crisis is exacerbated when her much younger personal assistant, Eve Harrington (Ann Baxter), steals her man, her Tony nomination, and nearly gets away with Margot's star quality, too. Fortunately, it takes more than a big hoopskirt to topple a drama queen like Margot, and she embarks on a full-frontal assault that proves that maturity, substance, honesty, not to mention four martinis on an empty stomach, will win out over youth and beauty every time. So if you're feeling like your personal sun is sinking slowly in the West, lash out with *All About Eve*, and let Bette Davis teach you how to rage—rage against the dying of the light.

QUOTABLE QUEENS

"I'll admit I may have seen better days . . .
but I'm still not to be had for the price of a cocktail,
like a salted peanut."

....

"Everybody has a heart—except some people."

....

"Oh, I'm sorry, I'm being rude, aren't I?
Or should I say, ain't I?"

....

"Remind me to tell you about the time I looked
into the heart of an artichoke."

BETTE DAVIS
AS MARGOT CHANNING IN *ALL ABOUT EVE*

QUOTABLE QUEENS

"I am big. It's the pictures that got small."

. . . .

"They took the idols and smashed them, the Fairbankses, the Gilberts,
the Valentinos! And who've we got now? Some nobodies!"

. . . .

"I'm rich. I'm richer than all this new Hollywood trash. Huh!
I've got a million dollars . . . own three blocks downtown.
I've got oil in Bakersfield. Pumping, pumping, pumping."

. . . .

"And I promise you I'll never desert you again because after
Salome we'll make another picture and another picture.
You see, this is my life! It always will be! Nothing else!
Just us, the cameras, and those wonderful people out there
in the dark! All right, Mr. DeMille, I'm ready for my close-up."

GLORIA SWANSON

AS NORMA DESMOND IN *SUNSET BOULEVARD*

. . . .

DON'T ASK, DON'T TELL:
QUESTIONS WE DON'T WANT ANSWERED

Norma: "My astrologist has read my
horoscope, he's read DeMille's horoscope."
Joe: "Has he read the script?"

GLORIA SWANSON AND WILLIAM HOLDEN

AS NORMA AND JOE IN *SUNSET BOULEVARD*

SUNSET BOULEVARD (1950)

STARS .... Gloria Swanson, William Holden, Erich von Stroheim

DIRECTOR... Billy Wilder

WRITERS .... Charles Brackett, Billy Wilder, D. M. Marshman Jr.

We all have people in our lives that cause us a little drama, but Norma Desmond (Gloria Swanson) holds the title for the drama queen of the silver screen.

Wrapped up in her own fantasy world, this no-longer-silent diva demands above-the-title billing from everyone around her, including her butler, her imaginary fans, her new lover, and even old Cecil B. DeMille himself. But as we and Norma discover, when we involve other people in our dramas, sometimes we wind up victims of our own tragic plot line.

Joe Gillis (William Holden) is silent-screen star Norma Desmond's newly hired writer slash houseboy. As Norma pulls Joe deeper into her private world, he's forced to give up his own, mostly because it doesn't fit in with Norma's design scheme. While Joe is working on Norma's epic disaster, however, he is secretly co-writing a movie of his own with the lovely Betty Schaefer, who doesn't demand star billing. Once the script hits the fan an enraged Norma takes things into her own hands (or rather her own pool) and proves that all the drama in the world can't buy you love.

So if you're getting caught in the crossfire, take cover on the couch, pop in *Sunset Boulevard,* and let Norma Desmond remind you of the very important lesson that all divas and partners of divas must learn—keep the drama on the screen, where it belongs.

THE PRINCE OF TIDES (1991)

STARS . . . . .Barbra Streisand, Nick Nolte, Blythe Danner,
. . . . Kate Nelligan, Melinda Dillon, Jason Gould

DIRECTOR. . . . . .Barbra Streisand

WRITERS . . . . .Becky Johnston, Pat Conroy (screenplay) ,
. . . . .based on the book by Pat Conroy

It's hard to imagine anyone stealing the scene when Barbra's around, but in this opera of domestic dysfunction it's Tom Wingo (Nick Nolte) who wins the drama-queen crown and reminds us all that if you want to command the spotlight, never ever try to perform opposite a wounded inner child.

Nolte stars as Wingo, a troubled man in mid-life crisis, who must confront the Lifetime movie of his abusive childhood when his twin sister attempts suicide in New York City. In an effort to unravel the mystery of his sister's mental illness, he strikes up a relationship with his sister's psychiatrist, Dr. Lowenstein (Barbra Streisand), and together they try to get right down to the real nitty-gritty of what makes a drama queen tick: perpetually reliving the trauma of the past in the present.

What begins as an attempt to give aid and comfort to Tom's talented but tormented sister, in very short order becomes a claustrophobic, anxiously attached, and codependent romance that is so all about Tom.

Of course, Lowenstein has a few dramas of her own—an unfaithful husband, a son who can't play catch—and she's sleeping with her patient once-removed, which is pretty edgy. There are a few scenery-chewing moments featuring Barbra's great gams and nine-inch nails. But in the end Babs is no match for Wingo, who drowns the stage in the muddy waters of long submerged emotion and reminds us all that Therapy is not just a gay bar on Fifty-second Street.

So if you're feeling pent up but afraid that you'll unleash an emotional tsunami, let *The Prince of Tides* remind you that sometimes it's silence that is truly deadly.

BEV'S HIDEAWAY AND LAUNDRETTE

FABRIC SOFTENERS FOR THE SOUL

If you're a little puffy around the eyes after a long night of high drama, turn those sour grapes into a morning-after mask, and restore your fluids for your next draining performance.

You will need:

- 1 handful green grapes

- 1 teaspoon boiling water

- 1 to 2 tablespoons powdered milk

Here's how you do it:

Smash the grapes until they are a mere shadow of their former selves. Strain the grape juice through a strainer and reserve the pulp. Add powdered milk and hot water until you've got a thick but spreadable paste. Cool to room temperature, then slather that stuff on your face and leave it there until it hardens, and for God's sake try to keep your mouth shut for at least twenty minutes or you'll crack the mask. Then wash the paste off with warm water and a moist cloth.

POOR ME, POOR ME, POUR ME ANOTHER

If you're in the mood to drown your sorrows, but you've got an early morning, pop in one of these "poor me, poor me, pour me another" movies, and let one of these infamous inebriated icons of the silver screen do the drinking for you.

WHO'S AFRAID OF VIRGINIA WOOLF? (1966)

STARS . . . . Elizabeth Taylor, Richard Burton, ... Sandy Dennis, George Segal

DIRECTOR . . . . Mike Nichols

WRITERS . . . . Ernest Lehman (screenplay), Edward Albee (play)

Nobody but nobody has done blousy and boozy quite like Elizabeth Taylor as Martha in Edward Albee's classic tale of a small-town university professor's wife and her one hundred-proof self-loathing, who manages to stagger her way through the long night of drunken delusion into the sober dawn of redemption, with a rocks glass in her hand.

From the very first gin rickey Martha is sipping her way toward a peach of a bun that's certain to shock the neighbors. Before she's through, Martha has managed to peel the labels off every bottle in the house, humiliate the host, horrify her party guests, and remind us that we are all afraid of Virginia Woolf, especially so after her fourth martini.

OUT OF THE MOUTHS OF BABES . . .

"You're all flops. I am the Earth Mother, and you are all flops."

. . . .

"I swear to GOD, George, if you EXISTED I'd divorce you."

ELIZABETH TAYLOR

AS MARTHA IN *WHO'S AFRAID OF VIRGINIA WOOLF?*

**"Martha, in my mind you're buried in cement right up to the neck.
No, up to the nose; it's much quieter."**

RICHARD BURTON

AS GEORGE IN *WHO'S AFRAID OF VIRGINIA WOOLF?*

**"I'm tired, I've been drinking since nine o'clock, my wife is vomiting,
there's been a lot of screaming going on around here!"**

GEORGE SEGAL

AS NICK IN *WHO'S AFRAID OF VIRGINIA WOOLF?*

"Ah, I hate all this love stuff, man. Wake me when the killin' starts."

. . . .

**"They say money can't buy you love.
The guy who said that was flat-ass broke."**

BETTE MIDLER

AS THE ROSE IN *THE ROSE*

THE ROSE (1979)

STARS .... Bette Midler, Alan Bates, Frederic Forrest

DIRECTOR .... Mark Rydell

WRITERS .... Michael Cimino, Bo Goldman (screenplay), Bill Kerby (story)

The Divine Miss "M" stars as The Rose, a Janis Joplin–inspired, sex, drugs, and rock-and-roll queen who can belt it out and booze it up like a Hell's Angel, but is really just a lost little girl looking for love in all the wrong places. And when she sings that love, it is a stranger, we're also reminded that after about six well bourbons and a coupla heroin chasers, everyone's a stranger, so it might be a better idea just to say no to the emotional crack.

WHATEVER HAPPENED TO BABY JANE? (1962)

STARS .... Bette Davis, Joan Crawford, Victor Buono

DIRECTOR .... Robert Aldrich

WRITERS .... Lukas Heller (screenplay), Henry Farrell (novel)

Bette Davis in a baby-doll dress. Joan Crawford in a wheelchair. Five bottles of gin, two bottles of scotch, one letter written to Daddy whose address is heaven above, and Victor Buono at the piano. Need we say more?

J A S O N ' S   B A R M A C Y

H O L L Y W O O D   H A N G O V E R   R E M E D I E S

So, you had a late night last night, huh? We know you want to get out of bed, if only the room would stop spinning right 'round baby right 'round. Go ahead, do that walk of shame to the kitchen and try one of these hangover remedies guaranteed to wake you up and remind you to take it a little easier next time around.

• Mix yourself up a packet of "Emer-gen-C" (from Alacer) with a glass of cold water, and chugalug Vanessa like you did last night!

• Eye drops, eye drops, eye drops!

• Eat fast food for breakfast. You need something to soak up all of that booze—something with a lot of fat, salt, and grease. It doesn't really help all that much, but you're bloated anyway, so why not live a little?

• Drink lots of water because you need to replenish those fluids and rebalance those electrolytes.

• If all else fails, wait twenty-four hours and don't forget to have more respect for your limits on the next boys' night out.

GIRL, INTERRUPTED (1999)

STARS.......Winona Ryder, Angelina Jolie, Brittany Murphy, Whoopi Goldberg

DIRECTOR..James Mangold

WRITERS................James Mangold, Lisa Loomer, Anna Hamilton Phelan,
....based on the book by Susanna Kaysen

If you're fed up with acting like a grown-up, and sick of following all the rules, let Angelina and Winona, two of Hollywood's most promising young drama queens, help you get in touch with the wild child within, without having to face an extended "rest" someplace upstate in the morning.

Susanna (Winona Ryder) is a lot like all of us fledgling drama queens. She both cares intensely and couldn't give a damn; she's pissed off at everyone around her, and desperately hungry for love. In other words, she's a little bit country, and a little bit rock and roll, and like many genre benders before her, is having some trouble combining all of the above into one musical variety hour.

When the ambiguity becomes too much for Susanna, she chases a bottle of aspirin with a fifth of vodka and winds up on a personal tour of the lockdown ward at Claymoore, a "home" for wayward girls, led by Whoopi Goldberg in a nurse's outfit. Now that is what we call a world-class walk of shame.

While at Claymoore, Susanna meets the outward manifestation of her inner angst, Lisa (Angelina Jolie), a primal scream of a girl who elevates chain-smoking to the level of performance art and lives her life like a chorus of "Born to Be Wild" on a loop.

What ensues is a full-fledged battle of the drama queens, with both delegates vying for the title of Miss Electroshock Therapy, 1999. We won't tell you who wins, but we will give you a heads up to keep the volume control handy whenever anybody tries to mess with Angelina Jolie's kickstand.

ANGELINA'S ANISETTES

"If I could have any job in the world I'd be a professional Cinderella."

ANGELINA JOLIE
AS LISA IN *GIRL, INTERRUPTED*

"Razors pain ya, rivers are damp. Acids sting ya, drugs cause cramp. Guns aren't lawful, nooses give. Gas smells awful, ya might as well live."

ANGELINA JOLIE
AS LISA PARAPHRASING DOROTHY PARKER IN *GIRL, INTERRUPTED*

"Talking about love is like dancing about architecture."

....

"I want to get rid of you as much as I want to get rid of that crap from Ikea."

....

"No, I heard what you said. And I'll admit 'What?' was a rather banal, cliché, non-colorful response. What I really meant to say was: 'Why don't you do the world a big fat fucking favor and crawl back into your mother's womb?' "

....

"Last time I saw Gary, he was wearing a blue sweater and a stupid expression. The sweater was new."

ANGELINA JOLIE
AS JOAN IN *PLAYING BY HEART*

WHEN YOU NEED A DOUBLE DOSE . . .

GIA (1998)

STARS . . . . Angelina Jolie, Elizabeth Mitchell, Faye Dunaway

DIRECTOR . . . . Michael Cristofer

WRITERS . . . . Jay McInerney, Michael Cristofer

If you're really in the mood to howl, do an Angelina double feature, and follow up *Girl, Interrupted* with Jolie's drama-queen debut in *Gia.* This made-for-TV biopic about seventies supermodel Gia Carangi, who scaled the heights of Studio 54 fabulousness only to plunge, Camille-like, into the grip of a substance abuse problem, unfolds like a Gaultier fashion spread circa 1984. It's a must-see. The dress is red, of course.

ANGELINA'S ANISETTES

"I do be da pittiest pittiest girl, I do be dat."

. . . .

"Look, this was a free trip to New York. If I had known you were looking for Marcia fucking Brady, I woulda stayed home."

. . . .

"Where's my knife? Who took my fucking knife? What do I look like, a fucking terrorist?! Is this funny? What the fuck is WRONG with you people?! Where the fuck—get the fuck away from me! GET AWAY! WHERE IS MY KNIFE?! [*crying*] God, you can't . . . you can't do that! You don't take somebody's knife when they need it!"

ANGELINA JOLIE
AS GIA IN *GIA*

HARRIET CRAIG (1950)

STARS . . . . Joan Crawford, Wendell Corey

DIRECTOR . . . . Vincent Sherman

WRITERS . . . . Anne Froelich, James Gunn (screenplay),

. . . . George Kelly (play, *Craig's Wife*)

World-class control queen Harriet Craig (Joan Crawford, who else?) is a woman passionately devoted to her possessions and rules her roost with a velvet fist. She's like June Cleaver on crack, and God help anyone who tracks in mud, breaks a vase, or puts his feet up on the coffee table. In fact, Harriet is so devoted to order in her home that she's willing to sacrifice anything or anyone that causes a ripple in the still waters of her outward appearance . . . like her husband's job, his friendships, and his peace of mind, for starters.

Harriet's husband (Wendell Corey) has given Harriet the wealth and social status that she so desires, but he also has the unmitigated gall to actually want to inhabit his living room. For this grievous untidiness, Harriet resents her husband deeply, and struggles valiantly to curb his masculine instincts lest they wrinkle the drapes.

Harriet's psychotic tidiness (which has the real La Joan with a capital "J" written all over it) eventually alienates her from everything human and warm in her life, including her faithful cousin, Claire, and, at last, her poor beleaguered husband—who smashes the porcelain vase of Harriet's flawless public persona—reminding us all that control queens often wind up ruling over an empty roost.

So if you've been white-knuckling the joystick of life and won't let anybody else near the controls, let Harriet remind you that sometimes cleanliness isn't necessarily next to godliness, and that a little bit of messiness is good for all drama queens who don't want to spend their lives playing to an empty, although very neat, room.

FOOTLIGHT FANTASIES: BECAUSE ALL DRAMA QUEENS HAVE TO BE SHOW-TUNE QUEENS SOMETIMES

LOVE! VALOUR! COMPASSION! (1997)

STARS .... Jason Alexander, John Benjamin Hickey, Stephen Spinella,
.... Stephen Bogardus, Randy Becker, Justin Kirk, John Glover

DIRECTOR .... Joe Mantello

WRITER .... Terrence McNally, based on the play by Terrence McNally

Are you sick of being the resident therapist in your circle of friends? Is it time to put the drama back on the stage where it belongs? Then it's time to step back behind the footlights and enjoy some love, valour, and compassion.

Gregory (Stephen Bogardus) invites six friends to join him and his boyfriend (Justin Kirk) for a long summer weekend. Eight gay men spending the summer in a secluded nineteenth-century country house sounds like fun, right? Throw in some infidelity, sickness, choreographer's block, and a fourteen-year anniversary (which we know in gay years is about fifty), and you've got one hell of a weekend.

So when your friends are driving you crazy, take a front-row seat and let the boys of Love! Valour! Compassion! teach you the importance of friendship, tutus, and love.

THE SHAPE OF WATER

"In this world, there is nothing softer or thinner than water.
But to compel the hard and unyielding,
it has no equal. . . . The weak overcomes the strong,
the hard gives way to the gentle. . . ."
LAO-TSE

"You must live in the present, launch yourself on every wave,
find your eternity in each moment."
HENRY DAVID THOREAU

"A ship in harbor is safe—but that is not what ships are for."
JOHN A. SHEDD

"You know what they say: You can lead a herring to water,
but you have to walk really fast or he'll die."
BETTY WHITE
AS ROSE IN *GOLDEN GIRLS*

AUDIOTHERAPY

TUNES FOR EVERY MOOD

When the drama in your life has hit critical mass, and you need to let off a little steam before you reach meltdown stage, listen to these belting divas tellin' it like it is!

"NO MORE DRAMA"
MARY J. BLIGE

"LAST DANCE"
DONNA SUMMER

"PUT THE NEEDLE ON IT"
DANNII MINOGUE

"MIDNIGHT TRAIN TO GEORGIA"
GLADYS KNIGHT & THE PIPS

"DON'T CRY OUT LOUD"
MELISSA MANCHESTER

"SHINE"
CYNDI LAUPER

CHAPTER THREE

JUST THE TWO OF US

Me-and-My-Girl Movies

There are times when nothing feels quite as good as curling up on the couch in front of the tube with your best girl who knows the song of yourself by heart and can sing it back to you when you've suddenly gone tone deaf.

If you're having one of those days when your hair's too big, your jeans are too small, and your tire is flatter than your stomach, put down your emotional winch, pick up the phone, and invite your one-woman support system over for a slumber party and celebrate the very special bond that only exists between women and gay men.

ROMY AND MICHELE'S HIGH SCHOOL REUNION (1997)

STARS . . . . Mira Sorvino, Lisa Kudrow, Janeane Garofalo, Alan Cumming

DIRECTOR . . . . David Mirkin

WRITER . . . . Robin Schiff, based on the play by Robin Schiff

When peer pressure is getting you down, there's nobody like your best girl, a pint of designer ice cream, and a couple of hours on the couch with Romy (Mira Sorvino) and Michele (Lisa Kudrow), the most lovable pair of bumbling gal pals to ever fold scarves on the silver screen.

In this classic blonde-leading-the-blonde tale, Romy and Michele have been the class outcasts basically since they entered school. With their idiosyncratic fashion sense and their total lack of self-awareness, not to mention that back-brace thing Michele had to wear through puberty, they were tormented by the elite of teendom with everything from insults to refrigerator magnets. But Romy and Michele never seemed to mind because they always felt cool so long as they were together.

Jump ahead ten years, and we find Romy and Michele still living blissfully in a cloud of cutting-edge denial, until it's time to venture back to Tucson for their big class reunion. Suddenly it dawns on them that maybe being unemployed, single roomies who can pinch an inch isn't so impressive after all.

And so they reinvent themselves, fashioning new figures, new careers, and new histories as if they were making new outfits, and venture back to their old dysfunctional stomping grounds to try out their new selves.

After a few public humiliations and one very long and somewhat disturbing interpretive dance number, our girls are airlifted out of the nightmare of adolescent self-doubt, and fly away on the wings of the knowledge that in the high school reunion of life, the prom crown goes to the queen who knows who she is and who her friends are.

TIT FOR TAT

Romy: "Actually, I have been trying this new fat-free diet I invented.
All I've had to eat for the past six days are gummy bears,
jelly beans, and candy corns."

Michele: "God, I wish I had your discipline."

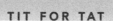

Romy: "Swear to God, sometimes I wish I was a lesbian."

Michele: "Do you want to have sex sometime to see if we are?"

Romy: "What? Yeah, right, Michele. Just the idea of having
sex with another woman creeps me out. But if we're
still single at thirty, ask me again."

Michele: "Okay."

MIRA SORVINO AND LISA KUDROW

AS ROMY AND MICHELE IN

ROMY AND MICHELE'S HIGH SCHOOL REUNION

DON'T DO IT: MOVIES THAT REALLY SHOULDN'T HAVE

THE NEXT BEST THING (2000)

STARS . . . . Madonna, Rupert Everett, Benjamin Bratt,
. . . . Malcolm Stumpf, Illeana Douglas, Lynn Redgrave

DIRECTOR . . . . John Schlesinger

WRITER . . . . Thomas Ropelewski

Madonna stars as Abbie Reynolds, a beautiful but unlucky-in-love thirty-something who accidentally becomes pregnant with her gay best friend Robert (Rupert Everett) one tequila-soaked night. Many Astaire and Rogers–inspired dance numbers, complete with period costumes and set appointments, ensue, followed by some first-class Hallmark moments between gay father and son, with mom looking on and glowing with a new millennium white light. The whole thing plays like an infomercial for alternative relationships, telling us that gay is okay, men and women really can be friends, friendship matters just as much as romance does, and love is love is love is love.

But, as is generally the case, trouble ensues when Mr. Right arrives. Metrosexual Ben (Benjamin Bratt) shows up looking very metrosexually available and starts doing a lot of really endearing straight guy stuff with Robert and Abbie's son, Sam (Malcolm Stumpf). And within a New York minute, Robert is shown the door along with his Judy Garland albums and ten years' worth of good parenting. Suddenly this alternative family is replaced with a good old traditional American nuclear furnace.

A legal battle ensues, and Ben and Abbie are awarded custody of Sam. But it's all right. Because in the end, in a *deus ex machina* that only Madonna would have the clout to pull off, Abbie decides not to move out of town, Ben turns down his partner track in favor of keeping the extended family together, and Robert gets really liberal visitation rights as well as the right to have Sammy call him "dad." This from the Material Girl, who owes her left Lear jet to gay guys and their best girls.

Okay, so like, first of all, respect and protect Madonna, okay? Condoms are always a good idea, even between best friends. And we're not too sure if impulsive pregnancy in response to aging issues is a step in the direction of health and happiness, but be that as it may . . . . We dare to wonder what might have happened if Abbie had decided to stick with Robert. Who knows? Maybe she would have gone on to star in her own network series, inspired a whole new generation of gay-friendly programming, and reminded us all that no genuine love between two people, gay or straight or in-between, is ever second-best.

THE BONDS OF FRIENDSHIP

"A friend may well be reckoned the masterpiece of nature."
RALPH WALDO EMERSON

"My true friends have always given me that supreme proof of devotion—a spontaneous aversion for the man I loved."
COLETTE

"It's the friends you can call up at 4 A.M. that matter."
MARLENE DIETRICH

"My mother used to say that there are no strangers, only friends you haven't met yet. She's now in a maximum-security twilight home in Australia."
DAME EDNA EVERAGE

"Each friend represents a world in us, a world possibly not born until they arrive, and it is only by this meeting that a new world is born."
ANAÏS NIN

PAGEANT PICS

When you're taking a break from the pageant of life, it's nice to be reminded that the crown still goes to the beauty queen with the best friends.

DROP DEAD GORGEOUS (1999)

STARS . . . . Kirsten Dunst, Ellen Barkin, Alexandra Holden,
. . . . Allison Janney, Denise Richards, Kirstie Alley

DIRECTOR . . . . Michael Patrick Jann

WRITER . . . . Lona Williams

Amber Atkins (Kirsten Dunst), the best little tapper in Mount Rose, Minnesota, takes on rich bitch Becky Leeman (Denise Richards) and her serial mom (Kirstie Alley) for the crown. A pyrotechnic illustration of white-trash values triumphing over upper-middle-class malice results, reassuring all of us teen princesses that in the pageant of life, a foundation of love and support—combined with a top-notch tap routine and a cute little cutaway—will win out over nepotism and a tasteless Christian interpretation of a Burt Bacharach ballad every time.

REALITY CHECK

Lona Williams, who wrote *Drop Dead Gorgeous*, made the local beauty pageant circuit before coming to Hollywood. Lona appears in the movie as Jean Kangas, Lester Leeman's put-upon secretary, and the silent and cringing Judge #3 in the Miss Mount Rose Pageant.

MISS CONGENIALITY (2000)

STARS ....Sandra Bullock, Michael Caine, Benjamin Bratt

DIRECTOR ....Donald Petrie

WRITERS............................Marc Lawrence, Katie Ford, Caryn Lucas

Special agent Gracie Hart (Sandra Bullock) goes undercover as Miss New Jersey in the Miss United States Pageant to expose a serial killer intent on blowing up the beauty queens. In order to get her man, however, tomboy Gracie must first go in search of her own inner beauty queen, and hires coach Victor Melling (Michael Caine) to undertake the challenge of his career and polish up her package. What we all learn in the end, however, is that the true measure of a beauty queen is not the size of her sash or the label on her gown, but whether she's willing to throw away a crown to save the life of her friends.

REALITY CHECK

The answer Cheryl, "Miss Rhode Island," gives to the question "What is your idea of a perfect date?"—"October 15"—was actually said by a contestant in a real beauty pageant. Who says you can't have beauty and brains?

BEAUTIFUL (2000)

STARS . . . . Minnie Driver, Joey Lauren Adams,
. . . . Hallie Kate Eisenberg, Kathleen Turner

DIRECTOR . . . . Sally Field

WRITER . . . . Jon Bernstein

Mona (Minnie Driver) is an alternative teen queen on a no-holds-barred mission to become the next Miss American Miss. Nothing, neither hell nor high water nor best friends facing murder charges without bail nor even an unexpected pregnancy, can keep Mona from her pursuit of the crown. But like all beauty queens, Mona learns in the end that in pageants, as in life, a crown is only worth as much as the person who wears it.

ONLY SKIN DEEP

"With one week to go before the pageant I was finishing my outfit, rehearsing my talent, and running 18 miles a day on about 400 calories. I was ready."

ALEXANDRA HOLDEN

AS MARY JOHANSON IN *DROP DEAD GORGEOUS*

"I'm Lorna Larkin, Miss Texas. I'm a *magna cum laude* graduate from the University of Texas with a double degree in genetic engineering and cosmetology."

BRIDGETTE WILSON

AS LORNA LARKIN IN *BEAUTIFUL*

FRIED GREEN TOMATOES (1991)

STARS .... Kathy Bates, Mary Stuart Masterson,
.... Mary-Louise Parker, Jessica Tandy

DIRECTOR... Jon Avnet

WRITER .... Fannie Flagg and Carol Sobiesk,
.... based on the novel by Fannie Flagg

Kathy Bates stars as Evelyn Couch, emphasis on the word "couch," an unremarkable housewife in crisis who is so desperate to get her husband's attention that she meets him at the door wrapped in plastic wrap. (P.S. He doesn't notice.) Sadly, somewhere along the meandering garden path of small-town southern life, Evelyn has lost all her mojo, and she is in dire need of an ab roller, a reliable estrogen replacement, and a best friend.

And as it usually happens in stories set in the rural South in quaint boarded-up cafés, life is cruel only to be kind, and Evelyn gets exactly what she needs, although not exactly in the form she expected. While on a trip with her husband to visit an ailing aunt in a nursing home, Evelyn meets Ninny (Jessica Tandy), an elderly southern belle with a lot of spice who tells Evelyn a story that literally changes her life.

Suddenly, Evelyn has something to look forward to and someone to love, and she returns to Whistle Stop each day to hear the next episode in the unfolding saga of Idgie (Mary Stuart Masterson) and Ruth (Mary-Louise Parker), two legendary best friends whose unshakable bond carries them through grief, prejudice, and more plates of pan-fried tomatoes and pork barbecue than you can shake a fork at. As she listens to Ninny's tale of sisterly bordering on Sapphic love, Evelyn begins to embrace her inner amazon, shed her excess baggage, and, with the help of her newfound friend, understand one of the most important secrets to happiness: though husbands and sons and lovers and friends may come and go, as long as you are able to love, there will always be love in your life.

SOUTHERN-FRIED WISDOM

"I found out what the secret to life is: Friends. Best friends."

JESSICA TANDY

AS NINNY THREADGOODE IN *FRIED GREEN TOMATOES*

"Secret's in the sauce."

CICELY TYSON

AS SIPSEY IN *FRIED GREEN TOMATOES*

"You a politician, or does lying just run in your family?"

"I don't know what's worse, church or jail."

MARY STUART MASTERSON

AS IDGIE THREADGOODE IN *FRIED GREEN TOMATOES*

BATES'S BEER NUTS

"I am a gay lesbian woman!
I do not mythologize the male sexual organ!"

· · · · · · · · · · · · · · · · · · ·

"Mr., I'm about to make you Mrs.!"

KATHY BATES

AS LIBBY HOLDEN IN *PRIMARY COLORS*

"Now, you listen to me, Mr. Grand High Poo-bah Bubba Buttcrack,
I'm about half-past give a shit. . . ."

KATHY BATES

AS DOLORES CLAIBORNE IN *DOLORES CLAIBORNE*

"Christ, anybody can be happy. Look at me, I laugh my ass off all the
damn time. You know, I'll laugh at just about anything."

· · · · · · · · · · · · · · · · · · ·

"You know, I never could stand people who keep sayin' they're gonna
go and then they never do."

KATHY BATES

AS STELLA MAE IN *COME BACK TO THE FIVE AND DIME,*
JIMMY DEAN, JIMMY DEAN

MY BEST FRIEND'S WEDDING (1997)

STARS .... Julia Roberts, Dermot Mulroney, Cameron Diaz, Rupert Everett

DIRECTOR .... P. J. Hogan

WRITER .... Ronald Bass

We all have a backup in case our dream love life fails us. But what happens when our backup falls out, too? This is the exact predicament that Julianne Potter (Julia Roberts) finds herself in when her best friend/backup Michael (Dermot Mulroney) announces his marriage.

It's not until Michael tells Julianne about his wedding plans that she realizes she loves him. Off she goes to Chicago to break up the engagement. When she meets Michael's fiancée Kimberly (Cameron Diaz), a sweet and guileless girl who immediately asks Julianne to be her maid of honor, Julianne must choose between her desire for Michael and her own better instincts. As usual, desire wins out and Julianne pulls out all the stops in order to call a halt to the wedding within three days. Realizing that she is racing against the clock, she sends for reinforcements. Enter gay best friend George (Rupert Everett), who tries to help Julianne realize that love doesn't necessarily mean having to say "I do."

CLUELESS (1995)

STARS .... Alicia Silverstone, Paul Rudd, Brittany Murphy,
.... Stacey Dash, Dan Hedaya

DIRECTOR .... Amy Heckerling

WRITER .... Amy Heckerling

In this modern retelling of Jane Austen's *Emma*, made back in the day when just about everything was a modern retelling of some Jane Austen novel or another, Cher (Alicia Silverstone) steps in as best friend and mentor to popularity-challenged Tai (Brittany Murphy) and, in the process of finding love for Tai, discovers that the man of her dreams has been standing right in front of her the whole time. In the end this movie counsels that maybe Cher would have recognized true love when it came along if only she wasn't so focused on looking for a designer label.

But as all of us truly clueless fans know, that kind of neo-Victorian anti-materialistic clap-trap is just a cover for what we all really want to see. In the end, this is a movie about hats and shopping and freeways and designer shoes. In a world of rising threats and plunging bottom lines, it's nice to remember that sometimes girls just want to have fun. You got a problem with that?

REALITY CHECK

In the classroom scene in *Clueless*, Alicia Silverstone really didn't know how to pro-nounce "Haitians" correctly, but the director liked it so much she told the crew not to correct Alicia, and it went into the movie.

During Cher's unsuccessful seduction scene with Christian in *Clueless*, they are watching *Some Like It Hot*, which is a film about Jack Lemmon wearing a dress, and *Spartacus*, which includes the famous scene where Laurence Olivier tries to seduce his houseboy, Tony Curtis. After a movie night like this, our gaydar would have definitely been tripped.

BEV'S HIDEAWAY AND LAUNDRETTE

FABRIC SOFTENERS FOR THE SOUL

The Beauty Bar

At your next girls' night, make a beauty bar. With just a few bowls of stuff you've got lying around the kitchen, you can create a beauty buffet for you and your gal that's guaranteed to enhance your inner glow.

You will need:

- 4 skinned, quartered, and pitted peaches
- 1 pint strawberries
- 1 cup instant oatmeal, prepared according to instructions
- 1 cup milk
- 1 cup sea salt
- ½ cup almond or grapeseed oil

Here's how you do it:

Place each of these ingredients in a separate bowl and mix and match to suit your mood. Mash up some peaches and add oatmeal for a peach-oatmeal mask, or soak a strawberry in milk and run it all over your face for a refreshing face peel. Saturate the salt in oil to make an exfoliant paste and then give each other a hand massage. Go ahead, don't be afraid to experiment. Mix and match the elements and see what you can come up with, because the best thing about beauty bars, gay men, and their best girls, is that we're not afraid to explore all of our options, and come up with combinations that no one ever thought of before.

BEACHES (1988)

STARS . . . . Bette Midler, Barbara Hershey, John Heard,

. . . . Spalding Gray, Lainie Kazan

DIRECTOR . . . . Garry Marshall

WRITERS . . . . Mary Agnes Donoghue,

. . . . based on the novel by Iris Rainer Dart

CC Bloom (Bette Midler) and Hillary Whitney (Barbara Hershey) meet one day on the beach, just two little girls with nothing in common. After years of mailbox friendship, the two find themselves living it up together in the Big Apple. Through love, romance, and lots of show-stopping Bette numbers, they realize that the love they so want from the men in their lives is the love they get from each other.

So when life is hitting your emotional overload button and the only solution is to bag a few rays with your best friend on the beach, let CC and Hillary remind you both to make new friends, but keep the old, because one is silver, and the other is, well, you know.

BETTE'S BAUBLES

"Oh, Harry, you're an angel. If your mother hadn't been such a bitch,
we could've shared something important."

. . . .

"But enough about me, let's talk about you . . .
what do YOU think of me?"

BETTE MIDLER
AS CC BLOOM IN *BEACHES*

"So, if I look like his mother and you look like his father, this is what
our son would look like. Pretty strong argument for birth control."

BETTE MIDLER
AS BARBARA STONE IN *RUTHLESS PEOPLE*

"I hate men who smell like beer and bean dip . . .
and makin' love in the back of recreational vehicles!"

BETTE MIDLER
AS SADIE RATLIFF IN *BIG BUSINESS*

AUDIOTHERAPY

TUNES FOR EVERY MOOD

Who better to crank up the beat and shake, shake, shake it with than your best gal? So the next time you two are all alone on the dance floor, pop in one of these tunes and celebrate love without borders.

"FOR ME AND MY GAL"
FROM *THE VERY BEST OF JUDY GARLAND*

"I SAY A LITTLE PRAYER"
DIANA KING, FROM THE *MY BEST FRIEND'S WEDDING* SOUNDTRACK

"THE LADIES WHO LUNCH"
FROM THE *CAMP* SOUNDTRACK

"I GOT YOU BABE"
FROM CHER'S *GREATEST HITS*

"CELL BLOCK TANGO"
FROM THE *CHICAGO* SOUNDTRACK

"EVERYBODY HAVE FUN TONIGHT"
WANG CHUNG, FROM THE *ROMY AND MICHELE'S HIGH SCHOOL REUNION* SOUNDTRACK

"DUETS" (ENTIRE CD)
FEATURING EMILY SKINNER AND ALICE RIPLEY

CHAPTER FOUR

SOMEWHERE OVER THE RAINBOW

Vicarious Party Pics for Landlocked Homos

If you love the nightlife and you've got to boogie, but the nearest gay bar is two states away and your budget won't cover a trip over the rainbow this weekend, don't despair. When your disco needs you, just pop in one of these Vicarious Party Pics for Landlocked Homos featuring some of the best bashes in technicolor history and follow the Yellow Brick Road to the Emerald City without ever leaving your own backyard. Also included are movies that will remind you that all that glitters isn't necessarily an emerald city, and, in the end, there's no place like home.

PARTY MONSTER:
THE SHOCKUMENTARY (1998/2003)

DIRECTORS...............................**Randy Barbato and Fenton Bailey**

The duo that brought us *The Eyes of Tammy Faye* do it again in this shockumentary, which takes us back to Disco 2000 and Club USA, and retells the story of how a club kid became a party monster, as told by the people who lived it, danced it, inhaled it, and snorted it.

Michael Alig left South Bend, Indiana, and came to New York City with big dreams and high hopes. He was attending Fordham and had a bright future as an architect ahead of him. But New York City nightlife and an obsession with "glamour" quickly drew him into deep waters. With his friend James St. James and club owner Peter Gatien, Michael created a club world of his own: a world full of sex, drugs, drag queens, and crack-addicted chickens. In their fabulous costumes, with their fabulous friends and, of course, their fabulous K, coke, X, and whatever else they could get their hands on, Michael, James, Peter, and their paid followers took New York by storm, throwing outlaw parties in subway stations and doughnut huts. It was all fun and games until Angel lost his wings and disco heaven turned into techno hell.

So when you're longing to crawl into that rabbit hole, slide down onto the dance floor, and not stop until you get enough, just make sure you locate your nearest emergency exit so that you can get out in case of a fire, because Michael never did.

CHICAGO (2002)

STARS . . . . Renée Zellweger, Catherine Zeta-Jones,
. . . . Richard Gere, Queen Latifah, Taye Diggs, Mya

DIRECTOR . . . . Rob Marshall

WRITERS . . . . Bill Condon,
. . . . based on the stage musical with book by Bob Fosse and Fred Ebb,
. . . . lyrics by Fred Ebb, music by John Kander

If you're in the mood to find a whoopee spot and maybe a little jazz hot, but you can't manage a trip to the Gold Coast this weekend, let Roxie and Velma lead you on a guided tour of sin city, where you can hear the music play and there's never a piper to pay, as long as you have a good defense attorney.

Okay, there's a plot here somewhere . . . something about multiple murders, and a mercenary attorney who exploits the public appetite for drama, turns the judicial system into a burlesque show, and sets murderesses free.

But the plot isn't really all that important. This is a movie about the American addiction to celebrity. It's about the Roxie in all of us who lives in a fantasy world bathed in the spotlight. Even from inside a prison cell she glows, accompanied by a rousing score, dressed in one of those sequiney little kick skirts and a lavaliere all the way down to her toes. Don't pretend that you don't know the name of the tune she sings. We've all whistled it a few times, okay?

But this movie is also about Velma (Catherine Zeta-Jones), the sadder but wiser non-blonde who has reached the top of the heap and means to stay there, and looks like she would kick some ass if anyone got in her way. And then, of course, there's Mama (Queen Latifah), who should be self-explanatory for a gay man.

But mostly, this movie is about partying with Bob Fosse, the original Billy Flynn, who infuses the world around him with razzle-dazzle and always provides a double dose of good but not-so-clean fun. So if you're itching to brush the sky, shake up a little bathtub gin, pull on your buckle shoes, pop in *Chicago*, and, for a couple of hours anyway, like the life you're living and live the life you like!

REALITY CHECK

Chicago is based on two actual murder trials that occurred in Chicago during the Roaring Twenties. Roxie Hart is based on a woman named Beulah Anna, a glamorous Chicago flapper who shot her lover, Harry Kalstedt, in cold blood because he announced he was leaving her. Afterward, Beulah hit the bathtub gin hard and played Hula Lou on her victrola. When the police arrived, although her husband vouched for her, Beulah was so blasted she confessed. She hired W. W. O'Brien, the real Billy Flynn who was famous for his high-profile manipulation of justice, to defend her. While in jail, she met Belva Gartner, the real Velma Kelly, a cabaret singer who had shot her married lover and then went out for cocktails. Velma's defense was amnesia due to excessive gin consumption. Both of these beautiful murderesses were acquitted by all-male juries, although everyone knew that they were guilty.

RAZZLE-DAZZLES

"I don't mean to toot my own horn, but if Jesus Christ lived in Chicago today and he had five thousand dollars, let's just say things would have turned out differently."

RICHARD GERE
AS BILLY FLYNN IN *CHICAGO*

CABARET (1972)

STARS .... Liza Minnelli, Joel Grey, Michael York

DIRECTOR .... Bob Fosse

WRITERS .... Jay Presson Allen, based on stories by Christopher Isherwood, ... the play *I Am a Camera,* and the stage musical .... with music by John Kander and lyrics by Fred Ebb

If you're in the mood for a wild night but don't want to leave the couch, put down the knitting, the book, AND the broom, and travel back to Berlin's Kit Kat Club in the thirties where the girls, the boys, and even the orchestra are beautiful . . . at least until they sound last call.

As *Cabaret* opens we are welcomed by the Master of Ceremonies (Joel Grey), who is as strangely androgynous as everyone else in this joint, which is a kind of twisted German 1930s Cheers—only with better lighting and less clothing.

Fresh-off-the-boat Brian Roberts (Michael York), who should be squeaky clean behind the ears and yet somehow isn't, stumbles into this strange café society and bumps straight into trouble. Spying fresh meat, Sally Bowles (Liza Minnelli) quickly pulls Brian into her life of fun, booze, Green Decadence nail polish, raw egg shooters, and heterosexuality. It's not long before Brian, who thought he was gay, starts getting a little confused (well, we are talking about Liza, after all).

When Sally winds up pregnant, Brian and Sally convince themselves for a few last precious hours that life is beautiful—that is, until the hobnail boots of reality kick in the door and remind all of us Kit Kat Club kids that no matter how much time you spend dancing to the music, you are eventually going to have to face it.

TRICK (1999)

STARS.....................Tori Spelling, Christian Campbell, John Paul Pitoc

DIRECTOR...Jim Fall

WRITER ....Jason Schafer

How can you get a date, a tour of New York City's West Village, and see Tori Spelling tap dance—all without leaving your living room? Watch the movie *Trick*, of course.

Gabriel (Christian Campbell) is your basic, run-of-the-mill, single, twenty-something show-tune queen. After yet another lackluster performance at his composer workshop, he ditches his best friend, off-off-off-off-Broadway baby Katherine (Tori Spelling), and heads to happy hour for some 'tinis and sympathy. Enter Mark, a beefed-up and gyrating go-go dancer out of Gabriel's wildest fantasies, whose nickname is not "Beer Can" because of his drinking habits.

Their eyes meet over Mark's G-string, and it feels just like love at first sight, but Gabriel can't find the courage to make his move; opportunity walks out the door, taking all the mystery lurking beneath that G-string with him.

Fortunately, this is a love story, and so fate intervenes, bringing these two ships in the night onto the same subway car, inviting nature to take its course. The only problem is, nature doesn't have an apartment in the city and a frantic search for a love nest ensues, with this modern-day Romeo and Romeo facing down all of the obstacles that stand in the way of instant-gratification love, like clingy best friends, straight-guy roomies, and bitter drag queens. If you're itching for a taste of big-city romance, but low on train fare, spend some time with the colorful characters of *Trick* and remember that in the big city, it's not what you know or where you go, but who has the key to an apartment not too far from an express stop.

REALITY CHECK

If you watch *Trick* really closely, you'll see your co-author, Jason, as the bartender (wearing the blue pleather shirt) in the go-go-boy scene in the opening moments of the movie. But be sure not to blink or you'll miss him!

STUDIO 54 (1998)

STARS...............Ryan Phillippe, Salma Hayek, Neve Campbell, Mike Myers

DIRECTOR ....Mark Christopher

WRITER ....Mark Christopher

Have you ever wondered what was behind the velvet ropes of Studio 54? Well, put on your flashiest ensemble and hustle back to New York City, circa early 1979, when the booze flowed like water and the lines inside were as long as the ones outside.

Shane O'Shea (Ryan Phillippe) is a nineteen-year-old gas station clerk in New Jersey, who dreams of a life of glamour in the big city across the water. With his boyish good looks and hot bod, Shane is picked by Steve Rubell (Mike Myers), the captain of the 54 ship, to come aboard. In no time, Shane is a 54 busboy rubbing elbows with the New York elite, even Julie Black (Neve Campbell), a fellow New Jerseyite who crossed the river into a soap opera career. Soon Shane is promoted to bartender, and his façade of a career takes off. With new-found friends and a new dream job, it seems the party will never wrap, but in this movie, as in life, all good things must come to an end. And when it does, you're gonna need a hell of a lot of Hefty Cinch Saks®.

When you're hungry for some disco and divine decadence, press your best groovy suit, get that disco ball swinging, and revel in a little "me generation" time at Studio 54.

IS THERE A COVER? MOVIE BARS WE'D LOVE TO GO TO FOR HAPPY HOUR

THE KIT KAT CLUB
FROM *CABARET*

Any place where Liza performs nightly and the drinks are as big as fishbowls sounds like our kind of gin joint. And how cool are those little phones on the tables? We'd suggest leaving before the mud wrestling begins.

THE MOULIN ROUGE
IN *MOULIN ROUGE*

There's no doubt about it—the Parisians really know how to construct a multi-media happy-hour experience, and the Moulin Rouge has got it all: Nicole Kidman in a beaded crown swinging from a trapeze; lots of exotically dressed and remarkably well-developed period extras; Christina, Lil' Kim, and Pink singing "Lady Marmalade"; and Ewan McGregor in a pair of knickers. Who could ask for anything more? Our only question is, Where the hell did they hide the bar?

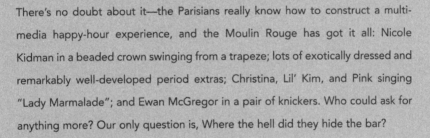

STUDIO 54
IN *STUDIO 54*

Been there. Done that. And the cover price is too high.

ODYSSEY 2001
IN *SATURDAY NIGHT FEVER*

John Travolta and his famous snake hips on a floor that lights up . . . 'nuff said. The only trouble is, we don't do outer boroughs.

DO THE HUSTLE: SPONTANEOUS DANCE NUMBERS THAT SO AREN'T

FROM JUSTIN TO KELLY (2003)

STARS..Kelly Clarkson, Justin Guarini

DIRECTOR...Robert Iscove

WRITER...Kim Fuller

We understand that a spring break teensploitation film starring the "American Idol" equivalent of Frankie and Annette, with characters sporting the most expansive array of cargo capris and spaghetti straps ever assembled on one beach blanket, is bound to inspire a few implausible dance numbers. But eleven of them? In eighty-five minutes?

FAME (1980)

STARS.................Debbie Allen, Anne Meara, Maureen Teefy, Irene Cara,
...................................Lee Curreri, Laura Dean, Antonia Franceschi

DIRECTOR...Alan Parker

WRITER...Christopher Gore

Okay, so we understand that there is going to be some spontaneous interpretive dance going on at a New York City high school for the performing arts. And when you've got a whole room of people who are learning to fly, there are going to be some tail feathers in the air from time to time. So we can understand a dance party or two breaking out in the hallways of Chorus Line High, but in a cab, in Bensonhurst, during rush hour?

FLASHDANCE (1983)

STARS.................................Jennifer Beals, Michael Nouri, Lilia Skala,
....Sunny Johnson, Kyle T. Heffner

DIRECTOR...Adrian Lyne

WRITERS...................................Thomas Hedley Jr., Joe Ezterhas

She's a steel worker by day, an exotic dancer by night, a ballerina in her dreams, and some-times at auditions she's a diminutive but remarkably muscular male break dancer when she gets to the hard parts. All this we can swallow, but what is with the impromptu pas de deux with the nautilus machines, complete with Olivia Newton-John let's-get-physical headbands, in a gym that boasts a scrim backdrop straight out of some minimalist, Bauhaus–inspired boutique design house in the sky? This stretched things a little . . . and we don't mean our hamstrings, okay?

BOOGIE NIGHTS (1997)

STARS...Mark Wahlberg, Burt Reynolds,
....Julianne Moore, Heather Graham

DIRECTOR...Paul Thomas Anderson

WRITER...Paul Thomas Anderson

If you're in the mood to party like it's 1979 but the nearest disco is two decades away, let Dirk Diggler and his enormous asset inspire you to get down and dirty without having to break out the emotional all-temperature Cheer in the morning.

Eddie Adams (Mark Wahlberg), a young and naïve Valley boy with delusions of grandeur that far exceed his high school equivalency score, is "discovered" in a club, where his true talents are hidden beneath a dishwasher's smock and a pair of Brittania jeans, which he'll unzip for five bucks a peek. Jack Horner (Burt Reynolds), a Larry Flynt–inspired pornographer only with a smaller cigar, recognizes a rising star when he sees one, and transforms Eddie into Dirk Diggler, the hottest young porn star on the late seventies circuit. And these were the Johnny Wad days, so that's saying a lot.

At first it seems that Dirk has got it all: sex, drugs, rock and roll, money, fast cars, a great seventies soundtrack, a world-class mullet, and the biggest liquid asset in the business. But then the future comes a-knockin' and takes all the swing out of Dirk's bat.

This journey to the dark side of Saturday night fever lets you dabble in the heady pleasures of the seventies when disco was king, drugs were non-habit forming, sex was safe, and denial worked, without having to face the Reagan eighties in the morning.

PEARLS FROM PORNOGRAPHERS

"When I close my eyes, I see this thing, a sign.
I see this name in bright blue neon lights with a purple outline and
this name is so bright and so sharp that the sign—it just blows up
because the name is so powerful. It says, 'Dirk Diggler.'"

....

"You're not the boss of me, Jack! You're not the king of Dirk!
I'm the boss of me! I'm the king of me. I'm Dirk Diggler! I'm the star!
It's my big dick, and I say when we roll!"

MARK WAHLBERG
AS DIRK DIGGLER IN *BOOGIE NIGHTS*

"I got a feeling that behind those jeans
is something wonderful just waiting to get out."

BURT REYNOLDS
AS JACK HORNER IN *BOOGIE NIGHTS*

"My wife has a cock in her ass in the driveway, all right?
I'm sorry if my thoughts are not on the photography
of the film we're shooting tomorrow."

WILLIAM H. MACY
AS LITTLE BILL IN *BOOGIE NIGHTS*

"I like simple pleasures, like butter in my ass, lollipops in my mouth.
That's just me. That's just something that I enjoy."

PHILIP BAKER HALL
AS FLOYD GONDOLLI IN *BOOGIE NIGHTS*

SUGAR SHACK
THE MAN-CANDY COUNTER

MARK WAHLBERG

PBH (Perpetual Bed Head), **RGSO** (Really Good Strap On), **LGICKBB** (Looks Great in Calvin Klein Boxer Briefs), **TPA** (Twelve-Pack Abs), **TEL** (Totally Endearing Lisp), **TSMFT** (The Sexy Minor Felon Thing)

TOP TESTOSTERONE PICS: *Renaissance Man, Boogie Nights, The Basketball Diaries, Rock Star, The Perfect Storm*

JOSH HARTNETT

RGH (Really Good Hair), **FSG** (Feckless Schoolboy Grin), **TSRRIHPT** (That Sexy Robert-Redford-in-His-Prime Thang), **WPBM** (Well-Positioned Beauty Marks), **LGIADT** (Looks Great in a Dog Tag)

TOP TESTOSTERONE PICS: *The Virgin Suicides, Blow Dry, Pearl Harbor, O*

JOHN TRAVOLTA

PBE (Piercing Blue Eyes), **TSST** (That Sexy Scientology Thang), **FSG** (Feckless Schoolboy Grin), **RGC** (Really Good Clefts), **TDEH** (Tendon-Defying Elvis Hips), **LGIG** (Looks Great in Grease)

TOP TESTOSTERONE PICS: *Grease, Carrie, Saturday Night Fever, Urban Cowboy, Blow Out, Pulp Fiction*

JOSH LUCAS

TSBCT (That Sexy Bill Clinton Thang), **PNE** (Paul Newman Eyes), **CC** (Chiseled Cheekbones), **WCD** (Way Cute Drawl)

TOP TESTOSTERONE PICS: *A Beautiful Mind, Sweet Home Alabama, The Hulk*

RYAN PHILLIPPE

RGC (Really Good Clefts), **EOTDBOY** (Emblematic of the Doomed Beauty of Youth), **TSST** (That Sexy Schoolboy Thang), **SIN** (Smoldering, Inscrutable, Noble), **LGIASOPB** (Looks Great in a String of Puca Beads)

TOP TESTOSTERONE PICS: *Little Boy Blue, I Know What You Did Last Summer, Gosford Park, Igby Goes Down, Way of the Gun*

CARRIE-ANN MOSS

STMS (Sexy Ten-Mile Stare), **RUM** (Raw Unpredictable Masculinity), **LGIAPS** (Looks Great in a Power Suit), **TSBLT** (That Sexy Bruce Lee Thang)

TOP TESTOSTERONE PICS: *The Matrix, Memento, Red Planet, The Matrix Reloaded*

LAURENCE FISHBURNE

MM (Major Mojo), **SAS** (Smooth as Silk), **TSOWKT** (That Sexy Obi-Wan Kanobi Thang), **LRGIATC** (Looks REALLY Great in a Trench Coat)

TOP TESTOSTERONE PICS: *Boyz N the Hood, Othello, The Matrix, Class Action, The Matrix Reloaded*

AUNTIE MAME (1958)

STARS . . . . Rosalind Russell, Forrest Tucker, Coral Browne,
. . . . Peggy Cass, Roger Smith, Jan Handzlik

DIRECTOR. . . . . Morton DaCosta

WRITERS . . . . Betty Comden and Adolph Green,
. . . . based on the play by Robert E. Lee and Jerome Lawrence,
. . . . and the novel by Patrick Dennis

Nobody entertains quite like Auntie Mame, Patrick Dennis's fabulous and forty-plus flapper, who drinks bathtub gin and joie de vivre in equal measure, and whose celebration of life reminds us that simply living is a good enough excuse to throw a party.

Mame (Rosalind Russell), a socialite in New York City in the Roaring Twenties, lives her life like one long happy hour with no last call, until her recently orphaned seven-year-old nephew, Patrick (Jan Handzlik), comes to live with her. Rather than reform her life, Mame sets about corrupting Patrick, introducing free love, bathtub gin, Freudian psychology, and monkey glands into his seven-year old lexicon. Soon, Mame and Patrick are taking on the establishment, creating theme parties wherever they go, and neither the Depression, nor widowhood—nor even a job in retail—can ring the last call bell on Mame's perpetual party.

So if you're feeling the need for a little Christmas right this very minute, pop in *Auntie Mame* and roll out the holly because it's always a holiday when there is joy in your heart.

WHEN YOU NEED A DOUBLE DOSE . . .

If you need an extra Mame fix, try the Gene Saks's musical version of *Auntie Mame*, called *Mame!*, starring Lucille Ball in a hoopskirt, supported by a kick line of surprisingly well-developed male period extras in red riding jackets . . . holding riding crops.

BEU'S HIDEAWAY AND LAUNDRETTE

THE BETTY FORD RECOVERY FACIAL

When you've been flirting with excess, this tough love facial will help restore your essential nutrients and emollients the morning after.

You will need:

- 1 skinned cucumber (cools and tightens)

- 6 strawberries (acts as alpha-hydroxy)

- ¼ cup honey (antibacterial)

- ½ cup yogurt (softens)

- ¼ cup milk (removes dead skin cells)

- 2 aspirin

Here's how you do it:

Take the aspirin with plenty of water, wait ten minutes for it to kick in, then throw the remaining ingredients in the blender and hit frappe. Pour half into a glass and half into a bowl. Slather the mixture in the bowl all over your face, then sit down, chill out, and drink the mixture in the glass with a little hair of the dog that hit you. The next time somebody offers you a third martini, remember this experience.

MOVIES THAT CHANGED DISCO

Sometimes a movie comes along that gets everyone's feet tapping to a new beat, and suddenly, the disco is never the same. Here are a few of our favorite groundbreakers that remind us all that if we can't dance, there's really no point in being part of the revolution.

SATURDAY NIGHT FEVER (1977)

STARS.....................................John Travolta, Karen Lynn Gorney

DIRECTOR...John Badham

WRITERS......................Norman Wexler, based on the magazine article
......................."Tribal Rites of the New Saturday Night" by Nik Cohn

Saturday Night Fever didn't just change disco, it created disco. From the moment bored American teenagers set eyes on this disco floor, it was love at first sight, and we all began strapping on our boogie shoes, and moving with the music, and refusing to stop until we'd had enough.

The story is a fairly simple one. Iconic Tony Manero (played by the iconic John Travolta before he hit the relaxed-fit stage), a nice Italian boy from Brooklyn who works in a paint store, lives his whole life for Saturday night when he rules the dance floor at the Odyssey 2001, and shows the world that he is not just another boy from the 'hood with a reliable blow dryer, but the undisputed king of disco.

Tony is content with his Saturday nightlife until he chooses Stephanie Mangano (Karen Lynn Gorney) to be his partner in the big dance-off. As they teach each other the steps, they also begin to learn that life is bigger than a disco floor, that Brooklyn is not the center of the universe, and that the coming-of-age classic that is their lives may very well inspire a sequel, as well as a Broadway musical.

Saturday Night Fever gave men permission to do a lot of things they'd never been able to do before, like wear platform pumps and white polyester leisure suits, and blow dry their hair. Most important, it allowed them to forget, if only for a few hours, the pressures of living in the morally ambiguous decade between the Summer of Love and the Reagan eighties, and just dance,

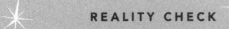

REALITY CHECK

Saturday Night Fever was based on an article by Nik Cohn called "Tribal Rites of the New Saturday Night," about a young store clerk named Vincent (the inspiration for Tony Manero) who lived to dance in a pair of platform pumps on the illuminated floor at the Odyssey 2001 in Brooklyn. Although Nik Cohn confessed much later that the Vincent in his article was totally made up, he had nevertheless captured what many of us young Americans were feeling at the time. When *Saturday Night Fever* was released in December 1977, it created a cultural earthquake that could be felt from Frisco to Chelsea. The Bee Gees's double album sold twenty-five million copies—more copies than any soundtrack before it—and featured ten hit singles. The disco industry flourished, gay bars multiplied, Studio 54 put up its velvet ropes, and platform shoes sold like hotcakes. Now that's what we call the good old days.

QUOTABLE QUEENS

"A mental mind fuck can be nice."

"It's not easy having a good time! Even smiling makes my face ache!"

"It was strange the way it happened. One of those quirks of fate. One of those moments when the chips are down, you're trapped, there's no way out and even if there was, it would probably be a one-way ticket to the bottom of the bay. Then you get a break! All of the pieces seem to fit into place. It took a small accident to make it happen. AN ACCIDENT! And that is how I discovered the secret. That elusive ingredient, that . . . spark that is the breath of life . . . yes, I have that knowledge! I hold the key to life . . . ITSELF!!"

TIM CURRY

AS DR. FRANK-N-FURTER IN *THE ROCKY HORROR PICTURE SHOW*

THE ROCKY HORROR PICTURE SHOW (1975)

STARS............................Tim Curry, Susan Sarandon, Barry Bostwick,
.....................Richard O'Brien, Patricia Quinn, Nell Campbell, Meat Loaf

DIRECTOR..Jim Sharman

WRITERS..................................Jim Sharman and Richard O'Brien,
...........based on the stage musical by Richard O'Brien (music, lyrics, book)

Dr. Frank-N-Furter (Tim Curry), the sweet transvestite from Transylvania, time-warped his way into the art houses of middle America and inspired all of us to take a few steps to the left.

When Janet (Susan Sarandon) and Brad (Barry Bostwick), two characters straight out of a wet dream of ideal suburban youth, break down on a lonely storm-swept road in the middle of the night, they are forced to walk to a nearby castle to use a phone. And, as this familiar Frankensteinian setup suggests, when the door to the castle is opened, they find more than just Ma Bell waiting for them.

From the moment Riff Raff (Richard O'Brien), the ghoulish butler who looks like Igor with a crystal habit, leads them into the cavernous halls of the manse lined with characters straight out of Studio 54 in the Liza years, Brad and Janet know that the Cheez Whiz is about to come off the cracker.

When Frank-N-Furter makes the scene, ascending, like the goddess of disco herself from the nether realms in a pair of platform pumps and a merry widow, vowing to make us a man in seven days, we know that the dance floor is never going to be the same.

This musical tribute to hedonism was nothing short of a cultural movement blurring gender lines in student union fashion from New York to Ashtabula, and elevated movies to the level of interactive performance art. But most importantly, *The Rocky Horror Picture Show* showed us that there's a disco queen inside each of us, and dressing her up in lingerie and lipstick and trotting her out onto the dance floor once in a while makes you more of a man.

CHAPTER FIVE

ONLY BACKWARD AND IN HEELS

Embracing-Your-Inner-Drag-Queen Movies

Are you beginning to feel like just another face in the crowd . . . just the third guy from the left in a pair of chinos and sensible shoes? Are you tired of blending into the chorus line of life and never once being the one to stand in the spotlight and belt out the money note?

If you're ready to stop being an ensemble player in the production number of your life, kick off those hush puppies, put on your dancing shoes, and pour yourself a little something pink and frothy. Then watch one of these Embracing-Your-Inner-Drag-Queen movies and let the notorious gender benders of the silver screen show you how to break out of your shell and exert a little creative control over your wardrobe and your life.

THE ADVENTURES OF PRISCILLA, QUEEN OF THE DESERT (1994)

STARS .... Terence Stamp, Hugo Weaving, Guy Pearce

DIRECTOR .... Stephan Elliott

WRITER .... Stephan Elliott

If you've been dying to take your act on the road, but you're worried about breaking down in the middle of an emotional outback, let the Queen of the Desert remind you that there ain't no mountain high enough to keep a cock in a frock with a rock from making it to the church on time.

Mitzi Del Bra (Hugo Weaving) is a drag queen down on her luck. She's deep in the throes of a mid-life crisis, increasingly annoyed with her sister act, and the only person who will hire her is her estranged wife, which, let's face it, isn't a very good résumé credit for any gender-bending cabaret chanteuse looking to take gay Sydney by storm. And maybe because she's ready for a spiritual walkabout, maybe because she wants to see her son and wife, or maybe because she can't figure out what else to do, Mitzi packs up the gowns, the feather boas, the backup divas, the Abba mixes, and together they hit the road.

Mitzi, Felicia Jollygoodfellow (Guy Pearce), and the transsexual Bernadette Bassenger (Terence Stamp) travel deep into the heart of the super-butch Aussie outback like easy riders (only in wigs and heels and with "Dancing Queen" rather than "Born to Be Wild" playing in the background).

Along the way the girls fight for truth, justice, and freedom of fashion, with only their sharp tongues and inner mettle for weapons. In the end, they remind us that the true measure of a man is not the size of his bus, or the credits on his résumé, or even the person on his arm, but his ability to pull off a crinoline strapless cut on the bias and a pair of platform pumps, and still get out of the desert alive.

DRAG-QUEEN DISH

"Why don't you light your tampon and blow your box apart,
because it's likely the only bang you'll ever get, sweetheart!"

....

"I've said it before, and I'll say it again: 'No more fucking ABBA!'"

TERENCE STAMP

AS BERNADETTE IN *THE ADVENTURES OF PRISCILLA
QUEEN OF THE DESERT*

"Oh, for goodness sake, get down off that crucifix,
someone needs the wood."

GUY PEARCE

AS FELICIA IN *THE ADVENTURES OF PRISCILLA
QUEEN OF THE DESERT*

"Being a man one day and a woman the next is not an easy thing."

TERENCE STAMP

AS BERNADETTE IN *THE ADVENTURES OF PRISCILLA
QUEEN OF THE DESERT*

....

REALITY CHECK

Priscilla originated the concept of "Dragarama," which meant that some inspired theaters that got caught up in the spirit of the thing hung a disco ball from the ceiling and flashed colored lights when the "Finally" dance number played on the screen.

When you need a prescription for extra-strength fabulous, try pairing up *Priscilla* with this American interpretation, which takes three straight actors, puts them in frocks, tosses them into a convertible with an unreliable clutch, and points them in the direction of Albuquerque.

TO WONG FOO, THANKS FOR EVERYTHING! JULIE NEWMAR (1995)

STARS......................Wesley Snipes, Patrick Swayze, John Leguizamo,
....Stockard Channing, Blythe Danner

DIRECTOR ....Beeban Kidron

WRITER ....Douglas Carter Beane

Miss Noxeema Jackson (Wesley Snipes), Miss Vida Boheme (Patrick Swayze), and Miss Chi-Chi Rodriguez (John Leguizamo) are all contestants in a New York City drag contest. Noxeema and Vida tie for first place and win a trip to L.A. to compete in the nationals. Miss Vida, being the good witch that she is, decides to take Chi-Chi under her feather boa and brings her along for the ride. So they pack up as much fabric, sequins, wigs, and dresses as their caddy can hold and venture off to L.A. Along the way they get stopped by homophobia, police harassment, and a bad carburetor, the last of which strands them in the armpit of America for two days in a roadside motel without a stitch of ambience.

So the girls set about creating their own sense of style deep in the heart of Middle America. They begin by teaching the local ladies how to enjoy a real day of beauty, New York style, and end up teaching the whole town what it means to be yourself.

When you're feeling the need for a virtual day-o-beauty, join the ladies of *To Wong Foo* and remember that fabulous is a state of mind.

QUOTABLE QUEENS

"When a gay man has way too much fashion sense for a single gender,

he is [*snap snap*] a drag queen."

WESLEY SNIPES

AS MISS NOXEEMA JACKSON IN *TO WONG FOO*

"I'm the Latina Marilyn Monroe.

I've got more legs than a bucket of chicken!"

JOHN LEGUIZAMO

AS MISS CHI-CHI RODRIGUEZ IN *TO WONG FOO*

"It's like my mother always said:

'Two tears in a bucket, motherfuck it.' "

....

"If y'see my life as I do, y'realize it's been one big metaphor for

that journey to the human state known as respect."

LADY CHABLIS

AS LADY CHABLIS

IN *MIDNIGHT IN THE GARDEN OF GOOD AND EVIL*

MIDNIGHT IN THE GARDEN OF GOOD AND EVIL (1997)

STARS .... John Cusack, Kevin Spacey, Jack Thompson,
.... Irma P. Hall, Jude Law, Lady Chablis

DIRECTOR.. Clint Eastwood

WRITERS .... John Lee Hancock,
.... based on the book by John Berendt

No setting produces characters quite like a cocktail party in the Gothic south, and the annual Christmas bash thrown by Jim Williams (Kevin Spacey) is no exception. In fact, his guest list is so colorful that it invites the attention of *Town and Country* magazine, which sends an unassuming, distinctly monochromatic reporter, John Kelso (John Cusack), to Savannah to cover the legendary shindig. And true to form, from the moment he steps over the Mason-Dixon Line, Kelso finds himself awash in local color. There's Jim Williams himself, a nouveau riche antiques dealer preoccupied with treasures and trash, as well as Jim's boyfriend, Billy (Jude Law), a metaphor for the place where sex meets violence. And then, of course, there's Minerva (Irma P. Hall), the bag lady who is blind but has perfect vision in her third eye, and some guy who wears a fly on a leash as a lapel pin. The brooch highlighting the décolletage of this antebellum murder mystery is the Scarlett O'Hara of the New South, Lady Chablis (played by . . . Lady Chablis), a self-described "big-mouthed drag queen" with legs as long as her story, and a personal code of ethics that she wears like a sunbonnet to shield herself from the scorching rays of Southern prejudice. While castles burn around her, as they do in the Old South, Lady Chablis stands tall and reminds us that when you're a black drag queen deep in Dixie, you'd better speak up, honey, and you'd better be tastefully accessorized when you do.

MRS. DOUBTFIRE (1993)

STARS . . . . Robin Williams, Sally Field, Pierce Brosnan, Harvey Fierstein

DIRECTOR . . . . Chris Columbus

WRITERS . . . . Randi Mayem Singer, Leslie Dixon,
. . . . based on the novel by Anne Fine

Let's face it. There are times in life when we all need a sassy-but-sweet sixty-year-old Irish drag queen to put us in touch with what's really important.

Daniel Hillard (Robin Williams) is a recently divorced, recently fired dad obsessed with holding on to his children, and frustrated that he can't see more of them. Well, this is, after all, a Disney movie.

When Daniel discovers that his ex-wife, Miranda (Sally Field), is looking for a housekeeper to help with the kids, he begins to think outside of the box. After his visitation rights become limited, he turns to his older, gay brother, Frank (Harvey Fierstein), for help. Uncle Frank dips into his costume trunk and contacts a few of his buddies in special effects, and before we know it, a very hairy, butch Daniel has been transformed into a very hairy, butch old lady called Mrs. Doubtfire.

But for some reason, everybody falls in love with Euphegenia Doubtfire, whose foam-rubber earthiness helps Daniel express his sensitive side. Daniel's kids and wife become very attached to their new housekeeper, but how will they cope when they learn that Mrs. Doubtfire isn't a Mrs. at all, but really just another side of dear old dad? Armed with a little ingenuity, and some very good structural undergarments, it's not long before Daniel and his whole family discover that it's not the clothes that make the man—when you want to draw people closer, all you have to do is be yourself.

So when you're feeling something precious to you slipping away, let Euphegenia Doubtfire remind you that it's not a wig and makeup you need to overcome life's obstacles, but courage and self-confidence, and maybe a good strong cup of English tea.

DRAG-QUEEN DISH

"My first day as a woman and I am already having hot flashes."

. . . .

"Isn't this posh? I'll bet you need credit
references just to get in the pool."

ROBIN WILLIAMS

AS MRS. DOUBTFIRE IN *MRS. DOUBTFIRE*

"You do an eclectic celebration of the dance! You do Fosse, Fosse,
Fosse, Fosse, Fosse! You do Martha Graham, Martha Graham, Martha
Graham, or Twyla, Twyla, Twyla, or Michael Kidde, Michael Kidde,
Michael Kidde, Michael Kidde, or Madonna, Madonna, Madonna,
Madonna . . . but you keep it all inside."

ROBIN WILLIAMS

AS ARMAND IN *THE BIRDCAGE*

BEU'S HIDEAWAY
AND LAUNDRETTE

BODY JEWELRY

You don't need to refashion yourself from head to foot to get a taste of what it means to be fabulous. All it takes is a few loose baubles, rhinestones, or beads—basically anything you can find that's smaller than a breadbox and glitters—and a little eyelash glue to transform you into an exotic empress of the East. Wear a red rhinestone between your eyes like a bindi or put rhinestones in the corner of each eye and really raise some eyebrows. Or if you're headed for a day at the beach, glue a sapphire in your navel to take your tan from day into night, and see if you don't mesmerize the boys of summer. All it takes is a little extra sparkle in your style to help you feel special. So the next time you're putting on the Ritz, experiment with a little body jewelry, and walk like an Egyptian.

THE QUEENS OF MACHO

The macho queens in these movies helped to expand our ideas about male fashion and taught us all that heroes aren't confined to suits of armor . . . sometimes heroes wear stilettos.

PERFORMANCE (1970)

STARS . . . . Mick Jagger, James Fox, Anita Pallenberg, Michèle Breton

DIRECTORS . . . . Nicolas Roeg, Donald Cammell

WRITER . . . . Donald Cammell

In this seventies tribute to the cinema of mind melt, Mick Jagger's rubber lips and rubber gender boundaries show us that just like neo-noir and sixties psychedelia, drag queens and hit men are just two ends of the same snake—and that real men really can wear lipstick.

Chas Devlin (James Fox), a hit man on the run in the classic macho, gritty British style, rents a basement in Knightsbridge from Turner (Mick Jagger), a fading pop star in a caftan surrounded by two androgynes (Michèle Breton, Laraine Wickens), a supermodel (Anita Pallenberg), and somewhere offstage, a very indulgent pharmacist.

Our macho neo-noir antihero initially reacts as one might expect to this group gender-bend, but after a few stiff belts of Turner's heady punch, this typical tough guy is sporting a bad wig and heels, and it's Turner who's packing the heat in pinstripes, and navigating the mean streets of sexual identification, where all the rules of alternate-side parking have been suspended.

QUOTABLE QUEENS

"The only performance that makes it, that makes it all the way,
is the one that achieves madness. Am I right? Eh?"

MICK JAGGER

AS TURNER IN *PERFORMANCE*

"Nothing is true; everything is permitted."

JAMES FOX

AS CHAS IN *PERFORMANCE*

"You are born naked—the rest is drag."

RUPAUL

"The world is changed because you are made of ivory and gold.
The curves of your lips rewrite history."

....

"Make a wish and see yourself onstage, inside out. A tangle
of garlands in your hair. Of course, you are pleasantly surprised."

EWAN MCGREGOR

AS CURT WILD IN *VELVET GOLDMINE*

"Man is least himself when he talks in his own person.
Give him a mask and he'll tell you the truth."

JONATHAN RHYS-MEYERS

AS BRIAN SLADE IN *VELVET GOLDMINE*

VELVET GOLDMINE (1998)

STARS .... Ewan McGregor, Christian Bale,
.... Jonathan Rhys-Meyers, Toni Collette

DIRECTOR .... Todd Haynes

WRITERS .... Todd Haynes, James Lyons

Bowie-esque pop star Brian Slade (Jonathan Rhys-Meyers) stages his own fake murder during a concert. Ten years later, journalist and former fan Arthur Stuart (Christian Bale) goes in search of Slade to prove that his favorite glam-rock star is still alive. But what he's really searching for is the cross-dressing androgyne within himself. And in the end, Arthur manages to resurrect Slade. Arthur dons a feather boa and reclaims his forgotten fabulousness. In the process he reminds us that there's a glam rocker in every macho man just dying to break free and lip sync.

AUDIOTHERAPY

TUNES FOR EVERY MOOD

When you feel the need to put on the pumps and break out the wig, pop in one of these drag favorites and lip sync your heart out, baby!

"THE TROLLEY SONG"
JUDY GARLAND

"IT'S RAINING MEN"
THE WEATHER GIRLS

"AND I'M TELLING YOU"
JENNIFER HOLIDAY WITH THE DREAMGIRLS

"LIZA WITH A 'Z'"
LIZA MINNELLI

"I LOVE THE NIGHTLIFE"
ALICIA BRIDGES

"MAN OF LA MANCHA"
LINDA EDER

"BELIEVE"
CHER

"DON'T LEAVE ME THIS WAY"
THELMA HOUSTON

THE KISS OF THE SPIDER WOMAN (1985)

STARS .... William Hurt, Raul Julia, Sonia Braga

DIRECTOR .... Hector Babenco

WRITERS .... Leonard Schrader,
.... based on the novel by Manuel Puig

What could be more macho than a bearded Raul Julia maintaining his silence in a South American prison? Why, his cross-dressing cellmate, of course, who is able to bend the bars of his cage and fight his way to freedom through the raw power of his imagination.

Valentin (Raul Julia), a passionate revolutionary with burning eyes, a resolute jaw, and a lot of hair on his back, is arrested as a political prisoner, brutally interrogated, beaten almost to death, then dumped in a cell to die.

Barely conscious and hovering near death, Valentin allows himself to be ministered to by his cellmate, a former window dresser named Luis Molina (William Hurt), who is in jail for "immoral behavior." Day by day, and all through the night, this alternative Florence Nightingale in a silk kimono and a pair of jeweled slippers nurses Valentin back to life with love, nourishment, and daily doses of the medicinal fantasy that has allowed Luis to survive his captivity—the narcotic kiss of the Spider Woman. The Spider Woman is Luis's beautiful and seductive female alter ego (Sonia Braga), who must decide whether she will betray the man she loves or sacrifice herself.

As Luis narrates each episode in his interior miniseries, he weaves a web of beauty, sensuality, and love whose strands are stronger than any steel bar.

P O L Y E S T E R (1981)

STARS ....Divine, Tab Hunter, Edith Massey, David Samson,
......................................Mary Garlington, Ken King, Mink Stole

DIRECTOR ....John Waters

WRITER ....John Waters

Drag queen extraordinaire Divine stars as Francine Fishpaw, a Barcalounger-sized soccer mom. When the neighbors discover that her upper-middle-class suburban utopia is supported by porn money, they begin picketing her split-level ranch and posting signs all over her corner lot. To make matters worse, her husband, Elmer (David Samson), who owns a chain of porn theaters, is cheating on Francine with his secretary. And if all this wasn't enough for a good, upstanding Christian drag queen to bear, Francine's daughter, Lu-Lu (Mary Garlington), gets knocked up by the bad boy next door, and her son, Dexter (Ken King), is a serial vandal.

So what's a cross-dressing queen-of-suburbia-in-crisis to do? Why, find a best friend called Cuddles (Edith Massey), of course, who recognizes and appreciates Francine's crown jewels. Then have a mad passionate affair with some hunk called Todd Tomorrow (Tab Hunter), and finally feel entitled to the kind of love, desire, and appreciation that a queen like Francine deserves.

So if you've been feeling like a pent-up and neglected housewife in a pre-fab hell of her own making, let Francine Fishpaw help you loosen that girdle, put down that feather duster, and access your inner Divine.

REALITY CHECK

The corpulent and courageous cult icon Divine grossed out America in John Waters's homage to American sleaze *Pink Flamingoes* when she ate dog poop on camera. Yes. Dog poop. After this auspicious launch into the popular dialogue, Divine became the most recognized and celebrated plus-sized male leading lady in Hollywood history, with such notable performances as the teen brat Dawn Davenport in *Female Trouble*, Edna Turnblad in *Hairspray*, and Francine Fishpaw in *Polyester*. Divine died in her sleep a week and a half after the opening of *Polyester*, but her courage and unyielding bouffant image live on in the hearts and stomachs of America as someone who had the balls to shock us all into taking a more honest look at ourselves.

DIVINE'S DIAMONDS

"All my life I wanted to look like Elizabeth Taylor.
Now Elizabeth Taylor looks like me."

"People who used to make fun are now fans. I had the last laugh."

"Of course the last thing my parents wanted was a son who wears a cocktail dress that glitters, but they've come around to it."

DIVINE

THE EYES OF TAMMY FAYE (2000)

STARS . . . . **Tammy Faye Bakker, RuPaul**

DIRECTORS . . . . **Fenton Bailey, Randy Barbato**

Okay, we know, Tammy Faye isn't really a drag queen. However, this perpetually perky, double-lashed bombshell of the Christian broadcasting world has a thing or two to teach us about insisting on your own special sense of fashion, no matter what kind of feedback you get out on the catwalk of life.

This documentary, narrated by RuPaul, takes an unflinching look at the mother of tele-vangelism whose eyes continued to glitter with the pure light of blind faith despite the encroaching shadows of her husband Jim Bakker's conviction, Jerry Falwell's hostile takeover, Jessica Hahn's *Playboy* confessional, eight hours in the Betty Ford Center for an Atavan addiction, and the demise of puppets as a central metaphor for the human condition.

Tammy's traveling drag show comes to an end in the middle of the Arizona desert, where this born-again Priscilla finds herself without a gig, a husband, a church, or a theme park. But Tammy doesn't turn into a pillar of salt. Instead, she teaches us the important lessons that her experience brings—when the going gets tough, the tough slap on a little Mac spackle and never get caught in the rainstorm of life without waterproof mascara.

TIPS AND FROSTS FROM TAMMY FAYE

"Yes. I have always loved lipliner! I like definition. It makes my lips pop. I guess I like pop all over! I mean, why blend it all in? If you're gonna blend everything in, why put it on in the first place?

"You can't go forward looking in the rearview mirror of your life."

"All in all, even if the film was not about me,
I would want to take time and go see it for the lessons it conveys.
I think everyone, especially young people, should see it
and realize that there is still life after tragedy
and that the human spirit is strong and resilient."

TAMMY FAYE BAKKER

T O O T S I E (1982)

STARS............................Dustin Hoffman, Jessica Lange, Teri Garr,
................................Dabney Coleman, Charles Durning, Bill Murray

DIRECTOR..Sydney Pollack

WRITERS.....................................Larry Gelbart, Barry Levinson,
................................Elaine May, Don McGuire, Murray Schisgal

Struggling actor Michael Dorsey (Dustin Hoffman) can't get cast to save his life, not even on soap operas, which are a far cry from the groundbreaking modern interpretations of Shakespeare's classics that he had imagined for himself. When his agent won't even return his calls and he's two steps away from boarding the Greyhound bus for home, he decides to do what many of us do when we're forced to think outside of the box—he finds a clingy red sequin gown, a pair of pumps, some reliable foundation, and heads out to set the world on fire.

When the camera focuses on Dorothy Michaels during her soap audition, everyone realizes that there is something remarkable going on, although nobody is quite sure what it is. The networks are initially horrified. But after the switchboard lights up with fans in response to Dorothy's debut, the networks realize that they have a first-class hit on their hands. Ironically, Michael Dorsey's feminine side commands a man-sized market share.

The only trouble is, the networks don't know that Dorothy Michaels is really a drag queen and neither does the soap's leading lady, Julie (Jessica Lange). Things get really sticky when Michael's inner white knight falls for Julie while still dressed up as his inner soap queen. It's a "Three Faces of Eve" thing.

And so, like Eve, Michael must face the question of integration versus compartmentalization. Does he want to be the fabulous soap queen Dorothy Michaels or the unemployed and love-sick actor who's fallen in love with an aging B-list soap opera actress who's in love with her chardonnay? Or will he find a way to do and be and have it all?

We'll give you one hint. *Tootsie* helped mainstream America understand that sometimes accessing your inner Dorothy is the best way to become a man. And there's nobody more macho than a pissed-off drag queen.

DOROTHY'S DIAMONDS

"Oh, I know what y'all really want is some gross caricature of a woman to prove some idiotic point that power makes a woman masculine or masculine women are ugly. Well, shame on you for letting a man do that or any man that does that! That means you dear! Miss Marshall, shame on you, you macho shithead!"

·························

"What kind of mother would I be if I didn't give my girls tits . . . tips?!"

DUSTIN HOFFMAN

AS DOROTHY MICHAELS IN *TOOTSIE*

REALITY CHECK

Dustin Hoffman, well known for his method approach to performances, was coached in the intricate art of female impersonation by Holly Woodlawn, the drag queen of Velvet Underground fame (Holly came from Miami, F-L-A).

Hollywood legend holds that the production crew on the set of *Tootsie* would only give bad news to Dustin Hoffman if he was in drag because they said he was a much nicer person as a woman.

WORDS TO LIVE BY

"If I'm wearing pants, call me a man. If I'm wearing a dress, call me a cab!"

HOLLY WOODLAWN

JASON'S BARMACY

THE PUCKER-UP MARTINI

As every queen knows, the sour apple 'tini is the way to go when you want a drink that's potent but tasty. Serve up this concoction in an extra big glass and pucker up, buttercup!

You will need:

- vodka

- "Pucker" sour apple mix

- green apple

- ice and shaker

- big-ass martini glass (big glasses make your hands look small, and other things look very large, especially after one refill)

Here's how you do it:

Mix two parts vodka and one part "Pucker" over ice, and shake the hell out of it until the vodka is bruised and cold. Slice the apple into fourths, then halve the quarters. Cut the apple slice vertically halfway up the middle and slide onto rim of glass. Empty the whole thing into the glass, serve to your favorite queen with your pinky extended, then smile, smile, smile!

CHAPTER SIX

CLEAN UP THIS MESS!

A-Boy's-Best-Friend-Is-His-Mother Movies

A boy's best friend is his mother. A boy's best friend is his mother. A boy's best friend is his mother. If you're hearing mom on a loop, put down the axe, pick up your remote, and take the edge off with one of these Mother-Issue movies. These homicidal screen moms will make your own mommie dearest look like Carol Brady by comparison, and comfort you with the thought that difficult though she may be at times, at least she's not Joan.

MOMMIE DEAREST (1981)

STARS . . . . Faye Dunaway, Diana Scarwid, Steve Forrest,
. . . . Howard Da Silva, Mara Hobel, Xander Berkeley

DIRECTOR . . . . Frank Perry

WRITERS . . . . Robert Getchell, Tracy Hotchner, Frank Perry,
. . . . Frank Yablans, based on the book by Christina Crawford

Nobody popularized egomaniacal, homicidal moms quite like Joan Crawford (Faye Dunaway), who rules her roost with a wire hanger and a pair of pruning shears, wearing the scariest facial goop ever slathered on a silent scream.

Joan Crawford is a shop girl turned movie star who worked her way to the top of the Hollywood heap the hard way, and took it out on her husbands, her adopted children, her housekeeper, and, ultimately, herself.

We first encounter La Joan in her pristine, white-on-white Brentwood mansion, where lint and independence are illegal, and where Joan's wishes are always fulfilled. So when she feels that something is missing in her perfect illusion, namely a child to make her life complete—Poof!—just like magic, a child appears, thanks to the behind-the-scenes efforts of her fairy-godlawyer and boyfriend, Gregg (Steve Forrest).

Young Christina (Mara Hobel), an orphan with blonde curls and blue eyes who looks like she walked straight out of central casting for the role of the angelic American child who will grow up to write a tell-all, is adopted into this control queen's castle. She's followed quickly thereafter by an equally ideal little boy, who spends most of his young life strapped to his bed, and who you can just tell is never going to be redeemed by a book or a movie deal because his sister will get to the well first.

What first appears like a dream come true rapidly turns into a nightmare. Throughout her childhood, Christina is held captive by the iron bars of Joan's expectations, struggles to live up to her mom's surreal standards, and tries to protect herself and her brother, Christopher (Xander Berkeley), from the hailstorms of Joan's ungovernable and unpredictable temper.

When teen Christina (Diana Scarwid) develops a will of her own, and starts getting a little tired of spending every Saturday night scrubbing the tiles of Joan's obsessive-compulsive disorder, things start to get campy. What ensues is a full-blown battle to the death between a mom who cannot let go, a daughter who will not be held, and a movie that doesn't know when to quit.

So if you've got a bad case of the Mom-is-driving-me-nuts blues, unplug the phone, pop in *Mommie Dearest,* and feel blessed, because things could definitely be worse.

REALITY CHECK

When Paramount first released *Mommie Dearest,* they thought they had a serious biopic on their hands. Audiences felt differently, and a month after the film was released some moviegoers (and we're not mentioning any names) started bringing Ajax and wire hangers with them to the theater, and turned *Mommie Dearest* into the interactive experience that it is today. Paramount, realizing they had another *Rocky Horror Picture Show* on their hands, began advertising the film as a camp classic, with the tagline, "Meet the biggest MOTHER of them all!"

RANTS AND RAVES

"I'm not mad at you, I'm mad at the dirt!"

· ·

"Christina! Bring me the axe!"

· ·

"Don't fuck with me, fellas. This ain't my first time at the rodeo."

· ·

**"I should've known you'd know where
to find the boys AND the booze!"**

· ·

**"No . . . wire . . . hangers EVER! What are wire hangers doing
in this closet when I told you: no wire hangers EVER?!!!"**

· ·

**"Ah, but no one ever said life was fair, Tina.
I'm bigger and faster. I'll always beat you."**

FAYE DUNAWAY

AS JOAN CRAWFORD IN MOMMIE DEAREST

WHEN YOU NEED A DOUBLE DOSE . . .

MILDRED PIERCE (1945)

STARS . . . . Joan Crawford, Jack Carson,
. . . . Zachary Scott, Eve Arden, Ann Blyth

DIRECTOR . . . . Michael Curtiz

WRITERS . . . . Ronald MacDougall, William Faulkner, Catherine Turner,
. . . . based on the novel by James M. Cain

If you're in the throes of major mom overload, and need a little extra punch in your antidote, hit the hard stuff with *Mildred Pierce,* featuring the real Joan Crawford. She caters a first-class guilt feast as this legendary doormat mom turned fast-food queen, who is victimized by her spoiled, selfish, thoughtless, ungrateful, and thoroughly heartless daughter Veda (Ann Blyth). Veda is probably the worst child ever portrayed on screen, without a single redeeming quality to her credit. Veda is content to enjoy the privileges of her mother's hard labor while looking down on her as a common waitress. And what's worse, she's constantly complaining about her mother's downscale decorating and bad fashion sense.

Add a faithless husband, the untimely death of her good daughter, and a bum murder rap to Mildred's heavy load, and you've got a masochistic-mom cocktail guaranteed to help you and your mom laugh away the icks and remind you both that in the world of moms and children, it's best to leave the blame game on the doorstep.

SHARPER THAN A SERPENT'S TOOTH

"With this money I can get away from you—from your chickens and
your pies and your kitchens and everything that smells of grease.
I can get away from this shack with its cheap furniture.
And this town with its dollar days, its women who wear uniforms,
and its men who wear overalls."

. . . .

"You think that just because you've made a little money
you can get a new hairdo and some expensive clothes
and turn yourself into a lady? But you can't, because you'll
never be anything but a common frump whose father lived
over a grocery store and whose mother took in washing."

ANN BLYTH
AS VEDA IN *MILDRED PIERCE*

WHITE OLEANDER (2002)

STARS . . . . Alison Lohman, Michelle Pfeiffer, Renée Zellweger,
. . . . Robin Wright Penn, Billy Connolly, Patrick Fugit

DIRECTOR . . . . Peter Kosminsky

WRITERS . . . . Mary Agnes Donoghue,
. . . . based on the novel by Janet Fitch

From the screenwriter who brought us *Beaches,* comes a mother-daughter melodrama that asks the questions, Where does a child end and a mother begin? and, How far down the road can you hold on to your mom's hand, without dead-ending in a cul-de-sac of codependence?

When Ingrid (Michelle Pfeiffer), a free-spirited and artistic intellectual, is jailed for poisoning her boyfriend with the deadly extract of her favorite white oleander, her daughter Astrid (Alison Lohman), is left to fend for herself in a system she was raised to despise.

Astrid, a mirror image of her mother's younger and less cynical self, is ferried from one foster nightmare to another in search of a place that she can call home. She spends some time with a born-again stripper called Starr (Robin Wright Penn), who introduces her to the comforts of spandex and Jesus. Next, there's Claire Richards (Renée Zellweger), a fading horror-flick star and the devoted wife of an absent husband, who teaches Astrid about real love and real good antidepressants. Unfortunately, the growing bond between Astrid and Claire doesn't sit well with Ingrid, who is rotting away in a cell plotting ways to keep Astrid as emotionally incarcerated as she is, hacking away at any new bonds Astrid forms, and consciously denying her daughter any chance at a life beyond the prison walls of her loyalty to her mother. Sound at all familiar?

And in an updated interpretation of *Lisa Bright and Dark,* emotional starvation gradually transforms Astrid from a blonde viking to a raven-haired version of Nancy Spungen in the Sid Vicious years. Will this sudden spectrum change at last alert Ingrid to the cost of her control, or will she maintain a death grip on her daughter's spirit all in the name of love?

When your mom has packed your bags and sent you on yet another unscheduled guilt trip, ease the load with a little *White Oleander,* and remember that in sufficient doses, even the sweetest flowers can be dangerously toxic.

PACK YOUR BAGS, YOU'RE TAKING A GUILT TRIP

"My mother was the most beautiful woman I had ever seen. She was also the most dangerous."

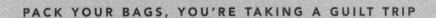

"You look at me, and you don't like what you see. But this is the price, Mother—the price of belonging to you."

ALISON LOHMAN

AS ASTRID IN *WHITE OLEANDER*

"I made you. I'm in your blood. You don't go anywhere until I let you go."

"Love humiliates you. Hatred cradles you."

MICHELLE PFEIFFER

AS INGRID IN *WHITE OLEANDER*

P S Y C H O (1960)

STARS .... Anthony Perkins, Janet Leigh, Vera Miles,
.... Martin Balsam, John Gavin

DIRECTOR .... Alfred Hitchcock

WRITERS................. Joseph Stefano, based on the novel by Robert Bloch

If you've been feeling tied up in knots by the old apron strings lately, and you're longing to cut the cord but you're afraid of what might happen if you pick up the scissors, let Hitchcock's famous ode to the Oedipus complex help you loosen the ties that bind, without having to serve twenty-five to life.

Norman Bates (Anthony Perkins), whose picture is now in the dictionary under "gay man's worst nightmare," tapped into all of our fears about the bad things that can happen when we can't say no to our mothers.

Stranded in a forgotten motel along a defunct highway, with only his stuffed birds and his mother fixation for company, Norman goes through the motions of his life, changing sheets and cleaning rooms, even though no one ever stays at the Bates Motel, and nothing in Norman's life is really alive at all. That is, until blonde, beautiful, and extremely animate Marion Crane (Janet Leigh) waltzes in with a trunk full of stolen booty and sporting the pointiest Playtex Cross Your Heart bra since Judy Garland. All of this forbidden blonde bodaciousness living and breathing within shouting distance of his mother sends poor Norman into a loyalty conflict between his devotion to his mother and his own tormented sexuality. And then, of course, Marion takes a shower, and mother sees red.

Aside from being one of the creepiest mother-issue movies ever made, Psycho is a great reminder that at least sometimes in life, disappointing your mother can be a good thing.

LAUREL CANYON (2002)

STARS . . . . Frances McDormand, Christian Bale, Kate Beckinsale,
. . . . Alessandro Nivola, Natascha McElhone

DIRECTOR. . . . . Lisa Cholodenko

WRITER . . . . Lisa Cholodenko

Jane (Frances McDormand), a fortysomething rock-and-roll producer who has made a career out of massaging ballads into the top ten, and massaging young male rock stars, too, isn't like any movie mom we've seen before. She wakes and bakes around noon, and then spends the rest of the day padding around her home recording studio with her newest boytoy, Ian (Alessandro Nivola). Afternoon quickly gives way to happy hour in Jane's Laurel Canyon home, where she paddles around her pool with a bunch of topless rock gods and more whiskey sours than you can shake a rhythm stick at. And when the night comes, she dabbles in a ménage à trois that includes her med student son Sam's fiancée, Alex (Kate Beckinsale). All before a nightcap at the Chateau Marmont. Now that's a mom we'd like to visit for the holidays!

REALITY CHECK

The white Ford that Marion drives in *Psycho* is the exact same car that the Cleaver family drove on "Leave It to Beaver." The license plate is ANL-709, which kind of puts Ward's starched collars and meticulous grooming habits in a whole new light.

FIRST WIVES CLUB (1996)

STARS . . . . Bette Midler, Goldie Hawn, Diane Keaton, Maggie Smith,
. . . . Sarah Jessica Parker, Dan Hedaya, Stockard Channing,
. . . . Victor Garber, Elizabeth Berkley, Stephen Collins, Marcia Gay Harden

DIRECTOR . . . . Hugh Wilson

WRITERS . . . . Robert Harling, based on the novel by Olivia Goldsmith

A thirst for revenge transforms three traditional moms into amazons with axes to grind. Best girlfriends Brenda Cushman (Bette Midler), Elise Elliot (Goldie Hawn), and Annie Paradis (Diane Keaton) get dumped for younger women, and then join forces to hit daddy where it hurts—smack dab in the bottom line. Toss in breaking and entering, embezzlement, and the hijacking of a window washer's scaffold and you've got some moms that we would definitely invite over for tea. But we'd be sure to lock up the breakables.

REALITY CHECK

Goldie Hawn, Bette Midler, and Diane Keaton were all born in the same year and within a month of one another. During the filming of *First Wives Club*, they celebrated their fiftieth birthdays together.

THE BANGER SISTERS (2002)

STARS........................Goldie Hawn, Susan Sarandon, Geoffrey Rush

DIRECTOR..Bob Dolman

WRITER..Bob Dolman

Lavinia (Susan Sarandon) is the picture-perfect doctor's wife, cradled in an upper-middle-class suburban utopia, until her old friend Suzette (Goldie Hawn) shows up and reminds Lavinia, and Lavinia's kids, what the "Vinnie" she remembers was really like. Lavinia's former bad girl within stands up and reclaims her flower power, shocking more than just the neighbors and reminding us all that inside every mom is a teenage wild child dying to do the frug one more time.

BAD HAIR BYTES

"I want to go out, but everything I own is beige."

SUSAN SARANDON

AS LAVINIA IN *THE BANGER SISTERS*

"I'm very sorry I ever met you. And I'm sorry that I allowed myself
to love you for all those years. I'm sorry that I did
nothing but be there for you every minute of every hour
and support you in your every MOVE. I'm sorry!"

DIANE KEATON

AS ANNIE IN *FIRST WIVES CLUB*

"You think that because I'm beautiful I don't have feelings.
Well, you're wrong. I'm an actress. I've got all of them!"

GOLDIE HAWN

AS ELISE IN *FIRST WIVES CLUB*

"Well, who plans on a change of plan? I mean, that would
be sorta paranoid, don't you think?"

FRANCES MCDORMAND

AS JANE IN *LAUREL CANYON*

THE GLASS MENAGERIE (1987)

STARS . . . . Joanne Woodward, John Malkovich, Karen Allen, James Naughton

DIRECTOR . . . . Paul Newman

WRITER . . . . Tennessee Williams

Nobody understood the excess baggage that gets hauled around by mothers and sons like Tennessee Williams. And *The Glass Menagerie*, Williams's ballad to a fading jonquil of the southern delta, and the son she puts in the place of the husband who fell in love with long distances, is perhaps one of the most disturbing depictions of what can happen when you have to say no to your mother.

Joanne Woodward plays Amanda Wingfield, a former Delta Queen, whose sensitive son, Tom (John Malkovich), dreams of life at the Palais de Danse and the colored lights of the disco ball. And because Tom spends his life dreaming of the homeboys of Guernica from his idle perch on the ramshackle fire escape of his mother's and sister's unhappiness, he constantly disappoints his mother. Tom isn't ambitious, he doesn't bring home enough money, he's too sensitive-looking around the eyes, he regularly forgets to pay the light bill, and he smokes. He also can't seem to come up with a viable suitor for his fragile sister, Laura, because the boys of Guernica just don't seem to be that interested in a stuttering metaphor for Tennessee Williams's survivor guilt. In the end, Tom, like many of us, must choose between saving his mother and saving himself.

So if your mom's been casting a shadow over your limelight lately, and you're ready to be the belle of the ball in the cotillion of your life, let Tom and Amanda Wingfield remind you that a son is a poor substitute for a husband or a reliable pension plan.

MOVIE MOMS TAKE ON SHOPPING

"Shopping really cheers a girl up."

MADONNA

IN *TRUTH OR DARE*

"I may be a beginner at some things,

but I've got a black belt in shopping!"

SHELLEY LONG

AS PHYLLIS IN *TROOP BEVERLY HILLS*

"The Virgin Mary speaks to me. She says, you must go to Tiffany.

And on the way, stop at Cartier."

SHARON OSBOURNE

IN "THE OSBOURNES"

"I don't want more choice, I just want nicer things."

JENNIFER SAUNDERS

AS EDINA MONSOON IN *ABSOLUTELY FABULOUS*

POSTCARDS FROM THE EDGE (1990)

STARS ....Meryl Streep, Shirley MacLaine,
.... Dennis Quaid, Gene Hackman

DIRECTOR ....Mike Nichols

WRITER ....Carrie Fisher, based on the book by Carrie Fisher

This fictionalized autobiography of Carrie Fisher's life stars Meryl Streep as Suzanne Vale, daughter of Doris Mann (Shirley MacLaine, who else), a famous screen ingenue turned gay icon in her dotage, who is loosely based on Debbie Reynolds. Doris is a turban-wearing, white-wine-swigging, over-the-hill matinee queen, who regularly breaks into song at casual get-togethers . . . you know, everything a guy adores in a mother but dreads in a lover.

Eventually, Suzanne can't stand the competition any longer—well, who could, darling—and after a fistful of pills, and a roll in the hay with yet another Mr. Right Now (Dennis Quaid), she buys a one-way ticket on the midnight train to Georgia and is rushed to the hospital, where a really handsome doctor who looks an awful lot like Mr. Right (Richard Dreyfus) pumps her stomach.

Will Suzanne rebuild her shattered life, stay sober, and, most challenging of all, find a way to cohabitate peacefully with her mother? Or will she inquire about the monthly rate at the local heartbreak hotel? We'll let you watch and find out for yourself, but we will tell you that from what we hear, the monthly rates at heartbreak hotels these days aren't much of a bargain.

MOVIE MOMS TAKE ON MANNERS

"Hey hey, Miss Penthouse '98, close those legs,

I could drive a boat show in there."

KIRSTIE ALLEY

AS GLADYS LEEMAN IN *DROP DEAD GORGEOUS*

"Losing one parent is unfortunate,

but two, now that's just carelessness."

JUDI DENCH

AS LADY BRACKNELL IN *THE IMPORTANCE OF BEING EARNEST*

"I did not lift my skirt, it twirled up! You only remember the bad stuff,

don't you? What about the big band I got to play at that party,

do you remember that? No, you only remember that my skirt

accidentally twirled up!"

SHIRLEY MACLAINE

AS DORIS MANN IN *POSTCARDS FROM THE EDGE*

"Chip, you know how I hate the brown word."

KATHLEEN TURNER

AS BEVERLY IN *SERIAL MOM*

"I feel like we should all sing one of those

lovely Christina Aguilera songs."

SHARON OSBOURNE

IN "THE OSBOURNES"

"It's like I always say,

if you don't have something nice to say

about someone, come sit by me."

OLYMPIA DUKAKIS

AS CLAIREE IN *STEEL MAGNOLIAS*

"Bad table manners, my dear Gigi,

have broken up more households than infidelity."

ISABEL JEANS

AS AUNT ALICIA IN *GIGI*

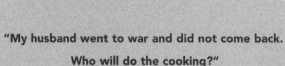

MOVIE MOMS TAKE ON MEN

"My husband went to war and did not come back.
Who will do the cooking?"

NICOLE KIDMAN
AS GRACE IN *THE OTHERS*

"Charlotte, I know you're planning a celibate life, but with half my
chromosomes, I think that might be tough."

CHER
AS RACHEL FLAX IN *MERMAIDS*

"When you love them, they drive you crazy,
because they know they can."

OLYMPIA DUKAKIS
AS ROSE IN *MOONSTRUCK*

"The men may be the head of the house but the women are the neck
and they can turn the head any way they want."

LAINIE KAZAN
AS MARIA IN *MY BIG FAT GREEK WEDDING*

"Had two husbands, one was too short, one was gay. Still, sweetie, if
you want to know how to peck a dwarf on the cheek as he's walking
out of the house to the disco in your dress, then I'm your girl."

JENNIFER SAUNDERS
AS EDINA MONSOON IN "ABSOLUTELY FABULOUS"

CARRIE (1976)

STARS . . . . Sissy Spacek, Amy Irving, Piper Laurie, Betty Buckley,
. . . . John Travolta, Nancy Allen, William Katt

DIRECTOR . . . . Brian De Palma

WRITERS . . . . Lawrence D. Cohen, based on the novel by Stephen King

Okay, being weird in high school is one thing . . . but when your mom is a big fundamentalist freak to boot, things can get messy.

No one knows this better than Carrie White (Sissy Spacek), a shy, fashion-challenged, and telekinetically enhanced teen, with a holy-rollin' mother who's well on her way to toontown. Poor Carrie—even getting asked to the prom by the class hunk lands her a beating from mom and a night locked in the prayer closet (and we thought *Mommie Dearest* was scary).

Miss Collins (Betty Buckley), a concerned gym teacher (hello), and classmate (Amy Irving) notice Carrie's silent plea for help and try to do what they can. With a prom queen crown, and newfound self-confidence, not to mention the pink prom dress she made herself, Carrie decides to grow up, confront her fears, and face down the Bride of Christ at home. But not before she brushes up on her telekinesis at the school library. So home Carrie goes, pins up Mom, and is off to the big prom where things, as so often happens when we say no to Mom and exercise our powers for the first time, get really messy. *Carrie* teaches us all a very important lesson about the cost of growing up and of ticking off somebody who can blow things up with her mind.

So the next time you're feeling locked in the mom closet, let Carrie, Carrie's mom, and Carrie's callous classmates remind you that reaching out with a hand of love is always better (and apparently safer) than pushing down with fear and hate in your heart.

GYPSIES, TRAMPS, AND THIEVES

These gypsies, tramps, and thieves are three of the top female gay icons of the twenty-first century. Not only are they singers, performers, directors, film stars, and authors, but surprisingly enough, they are all moms. Here are three of my favorite diva shows:

CHER: THE FAREWELL TOUR (2003)

No one is more versatile than Cher. Is that why we love her, or is it because she's the only one who can pull off 806 wig and costume changes in a one-and-a-half-hour show? Either way, this queen of change does it again in her three hundredth final farewell tour de force. With her Bob Mackeys as gaudy as ever; our favorite film, television, and show clips from yester-decade; and the only one with the ability to literally turn back time, we're certainly glad we got you, babe!

MADONNA: THE GIRLIE SHOW—LIVE DOWN UNDER (1993)

Our favorite boytoy does it again, only down under. Break out the bondage gear and the naked women descending on ropes—Madonna is back. Her first tour since Blonde Ambition and her last before motherhood, Madonna belts out all of our favorites with the costumes, half-naked dancers, obscenities, and favorite tunes we need and want to hear. From riding disco balls to American flag holidays, our Material Girl once again proves that she is nothing like a virgin. So, when you're feeling extra girlie, call up the boys, break out the headpieces, and watch Madonna go down under.

TIMELESS: LIVE IN CONCERT (2001)

Barbra does it again, this time for the millennium. She may be timeless, but our pocket-books had to be bottomless to afford these tickets. The concert opens with mini-Babs belting out "You'll Never Know" and, of course, big-Babs popping out of a cape for a rousing rendition of "Something's Coming." Barbra is in excellent voice for her three hundredth final farewell concert. With real Babs, mini Babs, and film-screen Babs all belting out together, who can help but be mesmerized (and pleasantly annoyed at times) by this one-of-a-kind instrument. Call up the boys, break out those secondhand clothes, and ring in the new year again and again with Babs and Babs and Babs.

CHAPTER SEVEN

WE'RE HERE, WE'RE QUEER

Inspiring-Your-Inner-Activist Movies

Are you mad as hell and ready to tell the world that you're not going to take it anymore, but you're afraid no one will be listening when the cat finally lets go of your tongue? Act up with one of these Inspiring-Your-Inner-Activist movies, featuring heroes who think globally, act locally, and change their corners of the world. They'll remind you that people really can make a difference, just by being themselves.

THE BOYS IN THE BAND (1970)

STARS . . . . Kenneth Nelson, Peter White, Leonard Frey, Cliff Gorman,
. . . . Frederick Combs, Laurence Luckinbill, Keith Prentice,
. . . . Robert La Tourneaux, Reuben Greene

DIRECTOR . . . . William Friedkin

WRITER . . . . Mart Crowley, based on the play *Boys* by Mart Crowley

Based on the play *Boys*, the off-Broadway taboo sensation that shocked New York in 1969, *The Boys in the Band* has a place in film history because it is one of the very first films to depict gay men living in their West Village world, doing what comes naturally. This movie also has the dubious distinction of featuring one of the worst cocktail parties in film history—which, granted, is hard to imagine with a room full of Chelsea boys, one of whom is a hustler in a cowboy hat. But when you're chasing your vodka stingers with *The Boys in the Band*'s brand of one-hundred-proof self-contempt, things can definitely get ugly.

Harold is having a birthday party, one of those numbers that comes after twenty-nine, which apparently was one of the seven deadly sins in gay Gotham way back when. To console himself, he invites his best friends over to commiserate. What ensues is a gay version of *Who's Afraid of Virginia Woolf?*, featuring the birthday boy as Martha, from whose acid tongue flows some of the best bitter queen banter ever written, but whose aftertaste is bittersweet. *The Boys in the Band* calls out from the past to remind all of us partiers of the future to hate ourselves a little less, and love each other a little more.

REALITY CHECK

The Boys in the Band cast members Kenneth Nelson, Leonard Frey, Frederick Combs, and Robert La Tourneaux all died of AIDS.

SAY IT LOUD, SAY IT PROUD

"Just by being out you're doing your part. It's like recycling.
You're doing your part for the environment if you recycle;
you're doing your part for the gay movement if you're out."

MARTINA NAVRATILOVA

"This sweet little blonde girl from 'The Sonny & Cher Show'
turned out to be a big dyke. There's something
wonderful about that, because that's life."

CHASTITY BONO

"I'm an openly gay trailer-trash Mexican.
How could they not love me?"

RUDY GALINDO

NORMA RAE (1979)

STARS . . . . Sally Field, Beau Bridges, Ron Leibman

DIRECTOR. . . . . Martin Ritt

WRITERS. . . . . Harriet Frank Jr., Irving Ravetch

There's nothing like Sally Field in a babushka and with a big old nit to pick to inspire us all to stand up and be counted.

In this ode to the power of one, perky textile worker Norma Rae (Sally Field), like her mother and grandmother before her, does the best she can to keep her head above water and care for her son, and find a new husband before she gets too old to kick her heels up at the local watering hole. And so the usual hum and whistle of her run-of-the-mill town life goes on until one day, quite unexpectedly, everything changes.

Reuben Warshawky (Ron Leibman), a recruiter for the Amalgamated Clothing Workers and Cloth, Hat and Cap Makers' Union, rolls into town and tries to convince the textile mill workers to stand up against years of mistreatment and poor wages and unionize. The only worker he's able to convince, though, is Norma Rae, who takes on her family, her friends, and her employers to make the world a better place for future generations.

And when little Miss Norma Rae, in that adorable apron with her jaw set just so and crowned by the above-referenced head scarf, holds up a sign that says "Union" as the machines shut down one by one in silent solidarity, you'll swear you've died and gone to I-can-make-a-difference heaven. So the next time you're feeling like you're just one little cog in a giant wheel, and no matter what you do you can't stop the wheel from turning, throw a chink into the works with *Norma Rae*, and remember, standing up for your own rights makes life better for everyone around you.

DON'T TREAD ON ME

"Forget it! I'm stayin' right where I am. It's gonna take you
and the police department and the fire department and
the National Guard to get me outta here!"

SALLY FIELD

AS NORMA RAE IN *NORMA RAE*

"It comes from the Bible:
'According to the tribes of your fathers, ye shall inherit. . . .'
It comes from Reuben Warshawky:
'. . . not unless you make it happen.'"

RON LEIBMAN

AS REUBEN WARSHAWKY IN *NORMA RAE*

REALITY CHECK

The movie is based on the true-life union-organizing campaign at J. P. Stevens Mill. The real-life Norma Rae is named Crystal Lee Sutton, who led the union campaign there. After Crystal and the workers won the election, it still took an additional ten years to get a union contract.

AND THE BAND PLAYED ON (1993)

STARS.........Matthew Modine, Alan Alda, Lily Tomlin, Charles Martin Smith,
.....................Richard Masur, Saul Rubinek, Richard Gere, Ian McKellen,
................................Anjelica Huston, Swoosie Kurtz, Steve Martin,
....Phil Collins, Glenne Headly

DIRECTOR...Roger Spottiswoode

WRITERS ....Arnold Schulman, based on the book by Randy Shilts

Randy Shilts's *And the Band Played On* is a groundbreaking made-for-TV exposé on the emergence of the HIV virus. While some consider this a dated and biased account, *And the Band Played On* put a human face not only on this deadly virus but on the gay community as a whole, and made a powerful statement about the power of one man to change the course of history.

Beginning with the emergence of a "gay cancer," which started killing gay men in alarming numbers in San Francisco, this documentary-style HBO miniseries follows CDC virus detective Dr. Don Francis (Matthew Modine) as he tries to halt the spread of this emerging global threat and confronts the administration that dared not speak its name.

Dr. Don Francis is joined in his struggle by Dr. Mary Guinan (Glenne Headley), Dr. Betsy Reisz (Angelica Huston), and Dr. Selma Dritz (Lily Tomlin) who track the virus from bar to bar and became responsible for the enactment of the legislation that finally closed the bath houses in San Francisco.

They are impeded in their race to put the genie back in the bottle by none other than the original bad boy, Ronald Reagan, who went for eight straight years, during the height of the spread of the disease, without ever once saying the word AIDS.

Dr. Don Francis is also hindered by the ego-driven medical-industrial complex, personified by one man, Dr. Robert Gallo, who withholds data, delays progress, and allows the disease to progress, so that he can claim credit for the discovery of the disease ahead of the French.

This movie is not only an up-close-and-personal look at the politics of our national response to an epidemic that targets gay men, but also an uplifting reminder that while one person can make a difference, a whole lot of people, joining together toward a common cause, can not only move mountains but maybe even a few right-wing politicians to boot.

REALITY CHECK

The filmmakers had to confront a lot of fear within the industry in order to make this picture happen. And it wasn't until Richard Gere accepted the small role of a gay choreographer inspired by Michael Bennett, that Alan Alda, Phil Collins, and Anjelica Huston were willing to attach their names to the project as well.

CAN I GET THAT PRINTED ON A PRIDE BANNER?

"This may be the first epidemic in history
of which no one officially died."

MATTHEW MODINE

AS DR. DON FRANCIS IN *AND THE BAND PLAYED ON*

QUESTIONS WE REALLY WOULD LIKE ANSWERED

"Isn't it a violation of the Georgia sodomy law for
the Supreme Court to have its head up its ass?"

LETTER TO *PLAYBOY* MAGAZINE, FEBRUARY 1987

BOWLING FOR COLUMBINE (2002)

STARS . . . . Michael Moore

DIRECTOR . . . . Michael Moore

WRITER . . . . Michael Moore

Crusader Michael Moore takes his one-man moral mosh pit on the road to investigate the roots of the Columbine tragedy. Looking down the barrel of an NRA-endorsed Glock, Michael Moore sets his sights on the lawyers, guns, and money that have seeped, like DDT, into our groundwater and poisoned our culture.

As Moore follows the trail of dollars, denial, and good old-fashioned middle-American defensiveness, he asks such difficult and compelling questions as: Isn't it dangerous for banks to give out firearms for opening an account? Does K-Mart have a limit on the number of bullets that people can purchase? Why do soybean farmers need automatic assault rifles under their pillows and napalm in their silos? Why did we really go to war with Iraq? Why did Charlton Heston take an NRA rally to Denver just three days after the Columbine tragedy, and just how many years have his hands been that dead and cold anyway? Why did anyone hate us enough to fly two planes into the World Trade Center? What does America's violent streak have to do with bowling, and what are we Americans so afraid of?

And while Michael Moore doesn't manage to provide answers to all of these disturbing questions, he does do the math for us and presents us all with a pretty sobering bottom line about the cost of deception, the wages of fear, and our national need for better anger-management skills.

With his usual shuffling yet searing and ironic style, this Woody Guthrie of the modern media gets to the very heart of America's preoccupation with guns and illuminates for us all the power of truth, and the way in which we can change the world, just by reaching out to one another with an open hand, rather than a trigger finger.

DON'T DO IT . . . SHOWS THAT REALLY SHOULDN'T HAVE

QUEER AS FOLK (2000)

CREATOR . . . . **Russell T. Davies**

Was anyone else as pissed off as I was when the first all-gay, slice-of-life show on television turned out to be nothing but soft porn about circuit boys behaving destructively?

First of all, I grew up near Pittsburgh and I now live in New York City and I've NEVER seen any clubs like the soundstage on "Queer as Folk." Not to mention the drugs, unprotected sex, and ridiculous instant relationships that are such a huge part of the lives of these "everyday gays."

There are some soft moments between these "friends," and we love the P.F.L.A.G. mom (who is a bit over the top), but why does it all have to be clouded with such nonsense and obviousness dressed up in chaps and set to a disco beat?

I wish these filmmakers would have the courage to show America that people in the gay community lead everyday lives, with the same wants, desires, and needs as everyone else. Every community and group has its own underbelly, but do we really want to be defined by it? That is why I say to "Queer As Folk," "Don't do it!"

CAN I HAVE THAT PRINTED ON A PRIDE BANNER?

"I don't mind straight people as long as they act gay in public."
T-SHIRT WORN BY DENNIS RODMAN

BEV'S HIDEAWAY AND LAUNDRETTE

FABRIC SOFTENERS FOR THE SOUL

If your dogs are barking from another hard day standing your ground, pamper your feet with this soothing soak, and rejuvenate yourself for your next freedom march.

You will need:

- 1 gallon of hot water in a bowl
- ½ cup Epsom salt
- ½ cup sea salt
- 1 teaspoon lavender oil
- 1 teaspoon peppermint oil
- ½ cup olive oil

Here's how you do it:

Fill a large foot basin or mixing bowl with water as hot as you can stand it. Dissolve Epsom salt and oils into the water, and soak your feet for at least fifteen minutes. Next, combine the olive oil with the sea salt and rub all over your feet. Then plunge your feet back into the basin to rinse off the oil; towel dry. You won't believe how smooth your feet will feel!

PHILADELPHIA (1993)

STARS......................Tom Hanks, Denzel Washington, Jason Robards,
....................Antonio Banderas, Mary Steenburgen, Joanne Woodward

DIRECTOR...Jonathan Demme

WRITER ....Ron Nyswaner

This was the first major studio release featuring box-office talent and an A-list director that dealt with the issue of AIDS, and forced mainstream America to realize that AIDS is a story that affects us all.

Based on a true story, Tom Hanks stars as Andrew Beckett, a top-flight attorney in a top-flight firm, in the top flight of Philadelphia society, who is fired by his homophobic boss, Charles Wheeler (Jason Robards), when it leaks out that Andrew has AIDS. What ensues has, by now, unfortunately become a familiar story. Andrew is unceremoniously escorted out of his professional life and deprived of his income, his medical insurance, and his dignity. But Andrew, whose health, but not spirit, is failing, resolves to fight back against injustice with whatever time and strength is left him. The trouble is, no one will represent Andrew against the most powerful law firm in Philadelphia, even though he is back-scored by a Bruce Springsteen ballad wherever he goes. Enter Joe Miller (Denzel Washington), a vaguely homophobic and ambitious young lawyer, who opens his heart and his mind to Andrew's circumstances and takes on the case.

Together with Joe, his lover, Miguel (Antonio Banderas), and his supportive family, Andrew spends his waning strength putting AIDS stigma on trial and tries to make the world a better place for those who will come after him.

This is a sad story, and some say, a dated one, but if you're feeling like one man can't fight City Hall, let Andrew remind you that no time is too short to strike a blow for compassion, brotherhood, and justice for all.

SILKWOOD (1983)

STARS .... Meryl Streep, Kurt Russell, Cher

DIRECTOR .... Mike Nichols

WRITERS.. Nora Ephron, Alice Arlen

In this true-life story, Meryl Streep stars as Karen Silkwood, a worker at the Kerr-McGee nuclear facility in Oklahoma, whose life takes a sudden turn when she is infected with radiation and unwittingly becomes the poster child for corporate negligence and irresponsibility.

Karen is a small-town girl, with small-town dreams and small-town sorrows—not to mention small-town employment opportunities. And her life is dominated by the rituals of small-town life: She fights with her boyfriend, Drew (Kurt Russell), and then has great make-up sex. She fights with her best girlfriend, Dolly (Cher, in her only role to date playing a lesbian), and then they console each other. She misses the son who lives with his father but tries to do the right thing going to work day after day after day at the Kerr-McGee plant that has employed generations in her small town.

And then one day, Karen sets the alarms off on the exit scan at the plant, and her life becomes a big-city nightmare. But for some reason, Karen doesn't lie down like generations before her and submit to an early grave, dug for her by industrial neglect. Instead, she joins forces with Paul Stone, a reporter from the *New York Times,* and tells the world about what is happening in her small town.

So if you're like a thrown rod in the nuclear reactor of life, let Karen Silkwood's bravery inspire you to fight back and make a difference, because every life is a terrible thing to waste.

REALITY CHECK

Hollywood legend holds that fifty-three gay actors appeared in *Philadelphia.* Within the next year, forty-three of them had died.

MAURICE (1987)

STARS ....James Wilby, Hugh Grant, Rupert Graves,
....Denholm Elliott, Ben Kingsley

DIRECTOR..James Ivory

WRITERS.................................Kit Hesketh-Harvey, James Ivory,
....based on the novel by E. M. Forster

This James Ivory period pic featuring two Edwardian gay men who fall in love is based on E. M. Forster's novel of the same name, which was the first novel involving a gay romance to have a happy ending.

Maurice (James Wilby) and Clive (Hugh Grant) are two English schoolboys who fall in love at Cambridge, and, in that brief window of time before social responsibility comes a-knockin', they enjoy a utopian summer romping through the poppy fields of the love that dares not speak its name.

But when fall arrives, the impossibility of their union catches up with them, and Clive, an aristocrat, assumes the mantle of landed gentry, and then marries a person more suited to his station—namely, a woman.

Maurice is, of course, miserable, and skulks around the hallways moping after Clive, clinging to his memories and the vain hope that Clive will change back into his true self. Maurice is inconsolable until he meets Alec Scudder (Rupert Graves), the brooding and mal-contented but incredibly hot gamekeeper, with that adorable accent straight out of Maurice's wildest forest fantasies, who can really fill out a pair of waders (and that's not even taking into consideration his very large shotgun—or his full game pouch). And we'll leave it to your imagination to figure out where Maurice finds his happy end.

So when you're ready to demand your happily ever after with the gamekeeper of your choice, tune into this groundbreaking E. M. Forster love story about living on the edge of seventeen in Edwardian England, a time when homosexuality was considered to be a dis-ease that you could cure with hypnosis, proper hygiene, and a healthy dose of denial. This movie will reassure you that as tough as things get nowadays, we've come a long way, baby, because of people like Forster and his hero Maurice, who had the courage to tell the world that they're happy just the way they are.

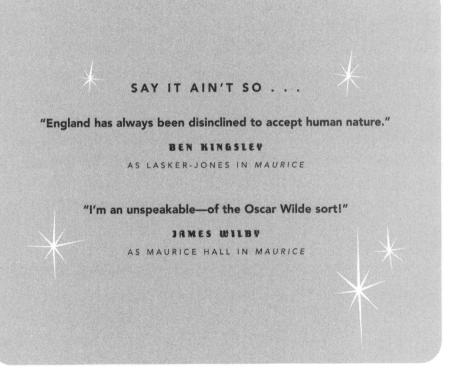

SAY IT AIN'T SO . . .

"England has always been disinclined to accept human nature."

BEN KINGSLEY

AS LASKER-JONES IN *MAURICE*

"I'm an unspeakable—of the Oscar Wilde sort!"

JAMES WILBY

AS MAURICE HALL IN *MAURICE*

MOVIES THAT CHANGED THE WORLD—
BECAUSE SOMETIMES A PICTURE IS WORTH
A THOUSAND WORDS . . .

THE TIMES OF HARVEY MILK (1984)

STARS .... Harvey Fierstein, Harvey Milk, Anne Kronenberg

DIRECTOR... Rob Epstein

WRITERS .... narration by Judith Coburn and Carter Wilson

This documentary, which became the first gay film to win an Academy Award in 1984, chronicles the early life and courageous career of San Francisco city supervisor and gay activist Harvey Milk. Milk, who was the first openly gay elected official in America, was assassinated along with San Francisco's mayor, George Moscone, by fellow council member Dan White, a former policeman and firefighter, and a real right-wing nut. From Harvey's early days as an affable and witty young man, through his passionate tenure as a pioneer in gay activism fighting to represent his growing gay constituency, this movie chronicles a short life well-lived. The loss to the gay community, which had finally found an ear and a voice in Harvey Milk, and the light sentence that his murderer received, sparked the White Night Riots in San Francisco and galvanized the gay civil rights movement. This movie is a telling and compelling portrait of a man whose unflinching honesty and courage in the face of adversity truly did change the world and reminds us that we can all make a difference just by telling the truth.

SILVERLAKE LIFE:
THE VIEW FROM HERE (1993)

STARS..Tom Joslin, Mark Massi

DIRECTORS......................................Peter Friedman, Tom Joslin

This landmark film exposed audiences for the first time to the painfully intimate, day-to-day ravages of AIDS from an up-close and hand-held vantage point. It changed the way the world viewed AIDS, death, and homosexuality. When filmmaker Tom Joslin's lover of twenty-two years, Mark Massi, was diagnosed with AIDS, Tom set out to create a diary of his lover's experience with the disease. Shortly after filming began, Tom himself sero-converted, and it turns out to be his death and not Mark's, that forms the climax of the movie. Shot on video (and later transferred to film) in a first-person diary style, *Silverlake Life* records the everyday struggle of lovers trying to keep living, loving, and expressing themselves, even as they are dying. The movie is an inspiration to all and a reminder that as long as there is life, there is hope.

REALITY CHECK

Dan White, who murdered Harvey Milk and George Moscone on November 27, 1978, avoided a first-degree murder conviction based on a "Twinkie" defense that claimed that he was suffering from an untreated depression, evidenced by an excessive reliance on sugary junk foods—namely Twinkies. In other words, the Little Debbie made him do it. The jury accepted this defense and convicted White of voluntary manslaughter. White received a seven-year sentence and was paroled in 1984 after serving only five years. Dan White returned to San Francisco, and on the morning of October 21, 1985, he attached a garden hose to the exhaust pipe of the family car and took his life. An Irish ballad, "The Town I Loved So Well," was playing inside his car when the body was found.

BOYS DON'T CRY (1999)

STARS . . . . Hilary Swank, Chloë Sevigny, Peter Sarsgaard,
. . . . Brendan Sexton III, Alicia Goranson

DIRECTOR . . . . Kimberly Peirce

WRITERS . . . . Kimberly Peirce, Andrew Bienen

Based on a true story, this Romeo and Juliet of the trailer park chronicles the short life of Brandon Teena, Teena Brandon (Hilary Swank), who hails from Lincoln, Nebraska, and feels more like a boy than a girl, and somehow finds the courage to do something about it.

Unhappy and misunderstood, she trades her frock for a sock in her jeans, and heads for Falls City where she presents herself as a boy for the very first time and meets the girl of her dreams, Lana (Chloë Sevigny). It seems at first that Brandon has found happiness at last, and he is, without question, the nicest boy in town. He's also a breath of fresh air for Lana, who is used to a town full of Joe Six Packs who still haven't learned that the measure of a man is not the size of his exhaust pipe. Unfortunately, Brandon's white-trash utopia is violently interrupted all too soon, when he's hauled off to jail on a warrant from home, and John Law discovers what's hiding—or rather, isn't hiding—inside Brandon's jeans.

What ensues is a graphic and brutal portrayal of hometown hatred, and the violence it engenders, but also a compelling portrait of the love that can develop between people who have the courage to tell the truth.

CAN I HAVE THAT PRINTED ON A PRIDE BANNER?

"No government has the right to tell its citizens when or whom to love. The only queer people are those who don't love anybody."

RITA MAE BROWN

SAY IT AIN'T SO . . .

"I don't know why anyone cares if I'm gay, and I don't know if it matters, or not. I just, uh, I don't—it's, you know, the whole aspect of coming out. I mean, there is a whole—people, you know, who are gay who have decided that it can be—that whole thing about calling people 'out'—and you have to share that, because there needs to be an equality and a lack of prejudice, and you need to have a voice. So, so, I mean, it's important, but I'm not involved in those dynamics and I have no point of view on it."

KEANU REEVES

"Oh my God, oh my God, oh my God. I am not a lesbian! I wish they'd stop saying it. I have a daughter, for God's sake."

WHITNEY HOUSTON

CHAPTER EIGHT

HOW CAN I MISS YOU IF YOU

WON'T GO AWAY?

Codependent Romances

We understand. We've all been through it. There you are, minding your own business . . . just another random, enchanted evening in a smoky downtown grotto with a piano bar, watered-down hooch, and poor ventilation. And then you see him, just another stranger with an umbrella in his drink across a crowded room. And the next thing you know, that stranger's initials are tattooed on your backside, his clothes are taking up way more than half of the closet space, his issues are occupying so much of your psyche that he ought to be paying rent, and he believes that a dish fairy comes in once a week to CLEAN UP HIS MESS!

If that fairy with the dishpan hands is you, pop in one of these Codependent Romances, about people who have made a far worse mess of things than you have and lived to tell about it. These movies will remind you that there is life after codependency, and you will survive!

IMMORTALITY (1998)

STARS . . . . Jude Law, Elina Löwensohn, Timothy Spall

DIRECTOR . . . . Po-Chih Leong

WRITER . . . . Paul Hoffman

If there's anybody worth climbing into a passive-aggressive pressure cooker with, it's Jude Law as Steven Grlscz, the emotional vampire with no vowels in his name, who lives on the feelings of others. It's like Steven himself is a word with no vowels—all tongue, and no breath—who gives drop-dead gorgeous a whole new meaning.

When we first meet the enigmatic and androgynous Steven, he is watching the police pull his fiancée's car out of a tree and dispassionately pondering the metaphorical implications of falling, without a drop of regret for his former dinner date whose life force slowly drips onto the forest floor, before his eyes.

Sound like your idea of a date from hell?

Well, but the thing is, it's Jude Law, don't you know. And more than that, it's Jude Law draped in satin and silk, and that weird parchment-paper caftan that whispers when he walks. It's Jude Law crouched, vulturelike, on a hillside at dawn, as the sun slowly illuminates his happy hunting ground, or gazing with an animal hunger into the heart of his prey. And it's Jude Law, sucking passion through a straw, like a margarita out of a hurricane glass, in a desperate attempt to quench his thirst for true love.

And so you call him back, don't you? You give him another chance, because even though he's a beast, you miss his Mona Lisa smile and that funny little button nose; that familiar dent in the pillow; and that adorable thing he has about using a mylar drop cloth, which won't absorb DNA evidence, as a mattress pad. Come on, admit it, you know you would so go out with him again. We would, too.

And so do all of the hapless Miss Lonely Hearts that Stephen fastens himself onto, like a lovely leech, and who wind up paying for the brush of his lips across their carotid with their lives. So if you're a feeling like a casserole dish on the buffet table of somebody's else's all-you-can-eat brunch, let Stephen Grlscz's insatiable appetites remind you to pick your dinner companions with care, lest you become somebody else's emotional entrée.

SINGLE WHITE FEMALE (1992)

STARS . . . . Jennifer Jason Leigh, Bridget Fonda, Steven Weber

DIRECTOR . . . . Barbet Schroeder

WRITERS . . . . Don Roos, based on the novel by John Lutz

Allison Jones (Bridget Fonda) has just gotten rid of her cheating boyfriend and is trying to enjoy her beautiful new apartment in New York's Ansonia. What is a single white gal to do all alone and new in the big city? Why, get a psychotic roommate of course (duh!).

Hedy Carlson (Jennifer Jason Leigh) is your normal mentally disturbed roommate. When Allison's boyfriend, Sam (Steven Weber), has an unexpected slap and tickle with his ex-wife, Hedy moves in with Allison, who starts her life of singledom. The girls lunch, shop, have day-o-beauties, and fix up their apartment, all things that are important in a time of healing and moving on. That is, until Allison takes Sam back and Hedy is left to fend for herself.

Hedy starts to borrow a few things from Allison—her clothes, her perfume, her boyfriend's life, her identity—you know, small stuff. Instead of calling the police or taking action, Allison tries to fix the sitch herself.

Allison and Hedy end up in a free-for-all, fight-to-the-death, basement battle of the crazies. So when you're feeling someone's codependence smothering your personal space, let the single white females teach you to take action, before it's too late. You may lose more than your beautiful new apartment.

BEU'S HIDEAWAY AND LAUNDRETTE

FABRIC SOFTENERS FOR THE SOUL

If you're feeling a little lifeless and brittle from all the shampoo it's taken to wash that man right out of your hair, try this deep-conditioning treatment for emotional split ends, and restore your bounce and luster.

You will need:

• 1 cup orange blossom or rose water

• 1 tablespoon carrot oil

• 10 drops vitamin E oil

Here's how you do it:

Combine ingredients, whisk until well-blended, and warm in the microwave. Pour the conditioner onto your wet hair, and then work into your hair and your scalp. Go ahead, massage the pressure points in your neck and temples the way that insensitive brute never bothered to. Then cover your saturated hair with plastic wrap and relax for an hour. Then rinse, shampoo, and rinse once more, and then toss your hair like a Breck girl. Look at you. You're gorgeous, darling. Well, it's his loss.

BITTER PARTY OF ONE: REVENGE-QUEEN MOVIES

When you've got an axe to grind, put down the hatchet, pick up your remote control, and let one of these famous revenge queens of the silver screen help you vent some of that pent-up angst, without having to face inflated insurance premiums in the morning.

SHE-DEVIL (1989)

STARS .... Meryl Streep, Roseanne Barr, Ed Begley Jr.,
.... Linda Hunt, Sylvia Miles

DIRECTOR .... Susan Seidelman

WRITERS .... Barry Strugatz, Mark R. Burns,
.... based on the novel by Fay Weldon

The husband (Ed Begley Jr.) of Roseanne Barr's plain old forgotten surburban mom, Ruth Patchett, takes up with Mary Fisher (Meryl Streep), a reigning pulp-romance queen, who dwells in a Pepto Bismol–hued paradise, where everything is rosy so long as Ruth doesn't find out. But Ruth does find out, and when she does, mousy Ruth, transformed by pure malice, becomes an avenging she-devil who reminds the world that hell hath no fury like a pissed-off housewife with a station wagon, your social security number, and a book of matches. Pure passive-aggressive caviar.

DOUBLE JEOPARDY (1999)

STARS .... Ashley Judd, Tommy Lee Jones, Benjamin Weir, Bruce Greenwood

DIRECTOR...Bruce Beresford

WRITERS....................................David Weisberg, Douglas Cook

We don't want to tell you too much, because the twists and turns that this movie takes are a big part of the rage ride, but we will tell you one thing: If you're in the mood to watch one pissed-off bitch take it out on the guy who done her wrong, then spend a couple of hours with Elizabeth Parsons (Ashley Judd), who reminds us all that no completely self-absorbed and insensitive, not to mention self-destructive, act ever goes unpunished.

PRICK UP YOUR EARS (1987)

STARS........................Gary Oldman, Alfred Molina, Vanessa Redgrave

DIRECTOR..Stephen Frears

WRITERS ....Alan Bennett, based on the book by John Lahr

The provocative life, startling career, and violent death, as well as emotional train wreck of a relationship that bracketed it all, is chronicled in this biopic of playwright Joe Orton. Beginning life as a shy, slight, and somewhat "theatrical" boy in the English midlands, Joe (Gary Oldman) manages to transcend his working-class origins and his complete lack of stage presence and win an acting scholarship to the Royal Academy of Dramatic Arts. And, as so many of us do, no sooner does he get a chance at the success he's always dreamed of than he hooks up with Mr. Dysfunction, Kenneth Halliwell (Alfred Molina), who is an even worse actor than Joe but dreams of being a writer.

Joe, unschooled in the finer things, sees in Kenneth a vision of all the sophistication he lacks, and soaks up all the instruction in literature and writing that Kenneth provides. Trouble brews when Joe becomes a better writer than his teacher and Joe's star begins to rise: he pens a hit on the West End, and even gets commissioned to write a script for the Beatles. Kenneth's sun begins to sink slowly into an ocean of insecurity, envy, and clinical depression.

Joe, bound to Ken by guilt, masochism, and frequent tours of London's public lavatories after midnight, begins a chain reaction that winds up causing a codependent nuclear meltdown.

Not only is this a compelling and beautifully told biography of a gifted, irreverent, and hilarious young writer who had the courage to tell the difficult truths to everyone but his boyfriend, but it is also a sobering reminder of the dangers of denial, and a reassurance that as bad as things might be getting in your artist's loft for two, at least when your boyfriend comes home, you don't have to hide the hammers.

SUGAR SHACK
THE MAN-CANDY COUNTER

HUGH JACKMAN

TIWL (That Irresistible Wounded Look), **SWHH** (Scary With His Hands), **RUM** (Raw, Unpredictable Masculinity), **LGIHAE** (Looks Great in Handcuffs and Epaulets)

TOP TESTOSTERONE PICS: *X2, Kate and Leopold, Animal Husbandry, Paperback Hero*

FAMKE JANSSEN

STMS (Sexy Ten-Mile Stare), **RUM** (Raw, Unpredictable Masculinity), **WCA** (Way Cute Accent), **LGIAPS** (Looks Great in a Power Suit), **TSBLIHPT** (That Sexy Bruce-Lee-in-His-Prime Thang)

TOP TESTOSTERONE PICS: *X-Men, I Spy, Don't Say a Word, Golden Eye*

STEVE ZAHN

RGH (Really Good Hair), **FSG** (Feckless Schoolboy Grin), **TSDWMCT** (That Sexy Dude-Where's-My-Car Thang), **LGIGG** (Looks Great in Geeky Glasses), **NATMW** (Not Afraid to Mud Wrestle)

TOP TESTOSTERONE PICS: *Reality Bites, That Thing You Do, Riding in Cars with Boys, Happy, Texas*

MISERY (1990)

STARS .... Kathy Bates, James Caan, Lauren Bacall

DIRECTOR... Rob Reiner

WRITERS.............. William Goldman, based on the novel by Stephen King

If your man has been threatening to run away and join the circus, and your arm is getting tired from hanging on to such a short leash, let Annie Wilkes teach you how a world-class drama queen keeps her rolling stone close to home, and remind you of the high cost of holding on while simultaneously reminding you of the high cost of holding on.

Best-selling pulp novelist Paul Sheldon (James Caan) takes a break in the North woods after finishing the last book in his blockbuster series, and putting his famous woman, Misery Chastain, to a final rest so that he can turn his attention to his "serious" novel. Which is just so like a man, isn't it? He abandons the one thing that has made him successful by killing off his loyal and trustworthy heroine, in favor of some ridiculous adolescent male fantasy about becoming Ernest Hemingway.

And, as is often the case with male mid-life fantasies, fate intervenes, and on a snowy road in the middle of nowhere, Paul runs himself into a snow bank and is badly injured, and somebody else has to pick up the pieces.

Enter Annie Wilkes (Kathy Bates), Paul's number one psycho fan, who rescues Paul from himself and teaches him a lesson about the price of success that he'll never forget.

Annie loves Paul, but she loves Misery even more. So while at first Annie nurses Paul gradually back to health with love, kindness, and a generous and refillable prescription for narcotics, when she discovers that Paul means to abandon Misery, things get ugly.

And as is usually the case when we try to hold on to something that can't be held, what ensues is a series of atrocities committed in the name of love that catapults this drama queen and her dream lover into a supernatural-thriller-sized battle to the death between yin and yang. Who will win? Paul or Annie? Celebrity or anonymity? Control or freedom? Manipulation or acceptance? Commercialism or conscience? Literature or pulp?

This is a great movie to watch when you're battling the immutable forces of inevitability.

Annie Wilkes's supernatural rage against the machine will help you vicariously vent a little of that pent-up angst. Then once you do, take a deep breath, put down the sledgehammer, open up your hands, and accept what comes or goes, because it will anyway, whether you want it to or not.

RANTS AND RAVES

"At the feed store do I say, 'Oh, now Wally, give me a bag
of that F-in' pig feed, and a pound of that bitchly cow corn?'
At the bank do I say, 'Oh, Mrs. Malenger, here is one big bastard
of a check, now give me some of your Christ-ing money!'?
THERE, LOOK THERE, NOW SEE WHAT YOU MADE ME DO!"

. . . .

"What's the matter? WHAT'S THE MATTER?!
I will tell you what's the matter! I go out of my way for you!
I do everything to try and make you happy.
I feed you, I clean you, I dress you, and what thanks do I get?
'Oh, you bought the wrong paper, Anne, I can't write
on this paper, Anne!' Well, I'll get your stupid paper
but you just better start showing me a little appreciation
around here, Mr. MAN!"

. . . .

"Now the time has come. I put two bullets in my gun.
One for me, and one for you. Oh, darling, it will be so beautiful."

. . . .

"He didn't get out of the COCKADOODIE CAR!!"

KATHY BATES

AS ANNIE WILKES IN *MISERY*

FIGHT CLUB (1999)

STARS............Edward Norton, Brad Pitt, Helena Bonham Carter, Meat Loaf

DIRECTOR ....David Fincher

WRITERS ....Jim Uhls,
......................................based on the novel by Chuck Palahniuk

This movie, which has the added benefit of featuring Brad Pitt AND Edward Norton engaging in human cock fights with their shirts off, is a movie that proves that it is even possible to have a codependent relationship with yourself.

Edward Norton and Brad Pitt star as Tyler Durden and his alter ego, two sides of the same codependent coin, who must battle it out with their bare knuckles in the boxing ring of Tyler's superego. Not surprisingly, this begins to cause some administrative hassles in Tyler's daily routines; for example, he beats up his boss, his apartment explodes, and he begins elevating homoerotic, sadomasochistic man-on-man action to the level of personal religion. And then, he falls in love. Will Tyler choose to stay in a bad marriage? Or will he break free from the abuser within, and just learn to say no?

If you're feeling like the punching bag in somebody else's fight club, let Tyler Durden remind you that when it comes to love, war, and support groups, it's better to walk away from the fight than to beat a dead horse.

WHEN YOU NEED TO CRY A RIVER: MALE PMS MOVIES

When it's been "that time of the month" all month long, and you're ready to shed a little of that excess irrigation, watch one of these male PMS movies, and weep away the bloat.

MOULIN ROUGE! (2001)

STARS......................Nicole Kidman, Ewan McGregor, John Leguizamo,
....Jim Broadbent, Richard Roxburgh

DIRECTOR ....Baz Luhrmann

WRITERS..Baz Luhrmann, Craig Pearce

Yet another young love plunges headlong into tragedy, only this time it's Nicole Kidman in forty pounds of beads and swinging from a trapeze. Now that's what we call progress. Satine (Nicole Kidman) is Paris's most famous courtesan and the star of the famous Moulin Rouge, Paris's notorious period hot spot (sort of like a nineteenth-century Limelight). The one rule of the Moulin Rouge, where sex, poetry, and reinterpreted rock ballads reign supreme, is never to fall in love. And so, of course, that's exactly what Satine and her young poet, Christian (Ewan McGregor), do. After a seduction scene in which Satine and Christian are so moved that they actually begin to converse in Elton John lyrics, they soar into the heights of love, back-scored by a revisited "Lady Marmalade" starring Christina, Li'l Kim, Mya, and Pink, only to have their disco paradise snatched away by consumption, gravity, and a complete lack of screen chemistry. Watch this one and weep over the cruelty of a world where not even Nicole in period lighting and a bustier can fool Mother Nature.

LOVE STORY (1970)

STARS .... Ali MacGraw, Ryan O'Neal

DIRECTOR .... Arthur Hiller

WRITER .... Erich Segal,
.... based on the novel by Erich Segal

Where do we begin to tell the story of how great a love can be? This is the sweet love story of a girl (Ali McGraw) who falls in love with a pre-law boy (Ryan O'Neal) and then drops dead before he even makes partner track, or gets the use of the company credit card. And nobody even says "I'm sorry." Now that's what we call a tragedy.

Ali McGraw stars as Jenny Cavalleri, a nice Italian girl from the neighborhood, who gets a scholarship to Radcliffe and falls in love with Oliver Barrett IV, who is a Harvard student, of course. After much sexually charged Harvard/Radcliffe ribbing, they fall in love and ultimately marry. Together they face the rigors of family disapproval, socioeconomic prejudice, first-year associate hours, infertility, and student housing. But together they make it through to the other side, only to be confronted at the finish line with a terminal bout of cancer, and several protracted and prosaic death scenes, not to mention an overwrought and overplayed theme song guaranteed to turn on the waterworks every time.

AUTUMN IN NEW YORK (2000)

STARS . . . . **Winona Ryder, Richard Gere, Anthony LaPaglia, Elaine Stritch**

DIRECTOR . . . . **Joan Chen**

WRITER . . . . **Allison Burnett**

It's the same old story: boy meets girl, girl develops terminal illness and kicks off right when things are starting to get interesting, boy learns his lesson about the quality and value of love. Tears and credits roll.

In this version of the familiar tale, Winona Ryder is Charlotte Fielding, a beautiful young milliner full of life and love, and really bad ideas about headwear that elevate hats to the level of performance art. He's Will Keane (Richard Gere), a successful restaurateur and playboy-about-town, who falls in love for the first time only to have it snatched away by the cruel forces of a studio bent on a New York version of *Love Story* with a leading man who's over twenty years older than the leading lady. But hey, he's Richard Gere, and he always brings us to tears.

LIFE WITH JUDY GARLAND:
ME AND MY SHADOWS (2001)

STARS . . . . Judy Davis, Tammy Blanchard, Victor Garber,
. . . . Hugh Laurie, Krista Sutton, Brandi Ward

DIRECTOR . . . . Robert Allan Ackerman

WRITERS . . . . Robert L. Freedman,
. . . . based on the memoir by Lorna Luft

If you're ready to weep a Swanee river, let Judy Garland's beautiful train wreck help put your trolley back on its track.

This made-for-TV movie starring Judy Davis as La Judy spans the entire epic tragedy of Judy's life from her Frances Gumm days spent tap dancing for peanuts on the Vaudeville stages of her mother's ambition, through the death of her father, five husbands, and addictions to as many pharmaceuticals as she could sew into the hems of her hoopskirts. Yet through it all—through fame and obscurity, love and loneliness, luxury and poverty, Liza and Lorna—Judy sang out and allowed us to cry with her and be healed by the magical power of her charmed voice.

JUDY'S JEWELS

"I've got rainbows coming out my arse."

. . . .

"Oh, for God's sake, Liza, can't you see I'm busy."

. . . .

"He adores me, and I need to be adored."

. . . .

"Since I was twelve years old they've been taking me out of the
closet and winding me up to sing and stuffing me back in again.
Well, maybe I don't feel like singing."

. . . .

"I'm only really at home in the spotlight."

AS JUDY GARLAND IN *LIFE WITH JUDY GARLAND:*
ME AND MY SHADOWS

CHAPTER NINE

I'VE BEEN TO P-TOWN, SOUTH BEACH, AMSTERDAM, IBIZA, AND THE GRAND CAYMANS, BUT I'VE NEVER BEEN TO ME

Finding-Yourself Movies

Have you been engaged in a transcontinental search for meaning, but all you've come away with is a lot of frequent flyer miles and a shoe box full of happy-hour receipts with numbers on the back? Are you beginning to wonder what it's all about, Alfie, and you'd ask him, too, only Alfie isn't returning your calls? Then watch one of these Finding-Yourself movies about people who have braved the bumpy road less traveled. Let these pioneers of the interior landscape help you discover a way to sing in tune with the melody of your own spirit.

ADAPTATION (2002)

STARS .... Nicolas Cage, Meryl Streep, Chris Cooper

DIRECTOR .... Spike Jonze

WRITERS .... Charlie Kaufman and Donald Kaufman,
.... based on *The Orchid Thief* by Susan Orlean

From the screenwriter who brought us *Being John Malkovich* comes another journey into the heart of the creative process that reminds us all that to truly understand anything or anyone else, we must first understand ourselves.

Nicolas Cage stars as Charlie and Donald Kaufman, the screenwriter and his identical twin. Charlie is an introspective and self-conscious writer who feels such reverence for *The Orchid Thief*, the non-fiction book that he is adapting to the screen, that he develops a near terminal case of writer's block. As Charlie spirals deeper and deeper into missed-deadline hell, his twin brother/alter ego, Donald, tries to help by offering lots of uncouth, unexamined plot suggestions that only serve to incense and paralyze his brother further. As an artist, and as a person, Charlie is Donald's identical opposite—a crass Hollywood crackerjack whose solution to everything in life and in art is to throw more sex, guns, and car chases into the equation. Whereas Charlie has too much reverence for the literary integrity of his subject, Donald has none at all and wants to transform everything in life or art into a formulaic action-adventure thriller.

These two creative visions go head to head in the primordial ooze of the Louisiana bayou, where John LaRoche (Chris Cooper) and the book's author, Susan (Meryl Streep), search for the rare ghost orchid, which is a kind of literary holy grail. Both artists and subjects pursue their elusive visions of beauty with the same single-minded determination, and all, on some level, are doomed to disappointment until they discover that the rare beauty they are searching for has been hiding inside themselves all along.

HEDWIG AND THE ANGRY INCH (2001)

STARS.................John Cameron Mitchell, Stephen Trask, Andrea Martin,
.................................Miriam Shor, Michael Pitt, Rob Campbell

DIRECTOR ....John Cameron Mitchell

WRITERS.......................John Cameron Mitchell, based on the play by
..................John Cameron Mitchell and Stephen Trask (music and lyrics)

Is it true that to be free you must give up a part of yourself? How far must we go to find that perfect love? Does it really take another person to complete us? These are all questions many of us have asked and Hedwig Robinson (John Cameron Mitchell) finds the answers in this amazing journey toward freedom and self-acceptance.

Hansel (John Cameron Mitchell) is a young boy from a broken home, coming of age in East Berlin when the Wall is going up. With the new love of an American G.I., and his mother's approval, Hansel undergoes a botched sex change and becomes Hedwig, a newly wed American citizen.

Stuck in rural Kansas with no friends, no husband, and no manhood, Hedwig does the only thing left to do: sing. As she sings her way across middle America following her rock-star ex Tommy Gnosis (Michael Pitt) in search of justice and answers, her story unravels.

When she finally comes across Tommy, they both basically implode and realize they are one and the same. So when you're stuck in a bus-and-truck tour of America's Denny's restaurants in search of yourself, let Hedwig and Tommy remind you that when searching for freedom and completeness, you don't have to look any farther than your own backyard, because if it isn't there you never really lost it in the first place.

KEEP THE RIVER ON YOUR RIGHT:
A MODERN CANNIBAL TALE (2000)

DIRECTORS . . . . **David Shapiro, Laurie Shapiro**

If the hubbub of modern life is drowning out your sacred sounds of silence, spend a few hours with seventy-eight-year-old gay anthropologist Tobias Schneebaum as he revisits the tribe of cannibals in Peru who turned him from a little-known painter into a world-famous anthropologist, but left him with hidden voices and painful memories still whispering to him from the jungle.

There's the rain and the mud that coats everything with a thin layer of silt, making river crossings treacherous for an elderly wanderer for whom a broken hip could mean never walking again. Then there's the joyful yet finite reunion with his former native lover and friend, Aipit.

And, finally, there is the Harakambut tribe itself, that years ago led Tobias into the wild heart of the jungle, simultaneously setting him free and ensnaring him. But despite the howls in the night, Tobias pushes forward through the mud and the memories, back to the bosom of the family that adopted him all those years ago, with whom he identified so profoundly that he even participated in their sexual ceremonies and ate human flesh, and was transformed from an urbane, hyper-civilized New York painter on holiday into a modern cannibal who would never paint again.

Along Tobias's trail through the Amazon Basin, we get a sometimes startling but always enlightening view of some of the most fundamental contradictions in nature: birth and death, age and youth, love and loss, humanity and brutality. Through Tobias Schneebaum's eyes we come to understand that even in the darkness, there is light; that in letting go we bring love closer; that in poverty there is wealth; in aging, youth; and in the grip of death, an embrace.

YOU CAN'T FOOL MOTHER NATURE

"I don't blame you for being scared—not one bit. Nobody with good sense ain't scared of white water."

HUMPHREY BOGART
AS CHARLIE ALLNUT IN *THE AFRICAN QUEEN*

"The adage 'blood is thicker than water' was invented by undeserving relatives."

RICHARD HARRIS
AS KING ARTHUR IN *CAMELOT*

"Get some sour cream and onion chips with some dip, man; some beef jerky, some peanut butter. Get some Häagen-Dazs ice cream bars, a whole lot; make sure chocolate, gotta have chocolate, man. Some popcorn, red popcorn, graham crackers, graham crackers with marshmallows, the little marshmallows and little chocolate bars and we can make s'mores, man. Also, celery, grape jelly, Cap'n Crunch with the little Crunch berries, pizzas. We need two big pizzas, man, everything on 'em, with water, whole lotta water, and Funyons."

JIM BREUER
AS BRIAN IN *HALF BAKED*

ELIZABETH (1998)

Stars . . . . Cate Blanchett, Geoffrey Rush, Joseph Fiennes,
. . . . Christopher Eccleston, Richard Attenborough

Director . . . . Shekhar Kapur

Writer . . . . Michael Hirst

There are times in life when, without warning, nearly everything changes. You go to sleep a princess dreaming about your newest puppy love and wake up queen of a religiously divided, bankrupt kingdom of drama, where even your advisors are against you. Don't you just hate it when that happens?

Elizabeth I (Cate Blanchett) is a queen who rules with her heart, not her mind. With too many cooks in her kitchen, Elizabeth immediately faces war and assassination. Her advisors tell her that marriage is the only answer. After a rocky start, Elizabeth looks within herself and her own conscience and heads start to roll, LITERALLY. With a trustworthy court and newfound confidence, Elizabeth becomes a virgin and rules for the next forty-five years, an era now called "The Golden Age" because she learned to listen to her own instincts.

So, when you find yourself in the dungeons of a new kingdom, let *Elizabeth* remind you that the only person that should be on your throne is you, and we have the power to change the world when we learn the courage of our own convictions.

QUOTABLE QUEENS

"I am not your Elizabeth! I am no man's Elizabeth!"

. . . .

"I will have one mistress here . . . and no master!"

. . . .

"I am my father's daughter. I'm not afraid of anything."

CATE BLANCHETT
AS ELIZABETH I IN *ELIZABETH*

AMERICAN BEAUTY (1999)

STARS...........................Kevin Spacey, Annette Bening, Thora Birch,
.....................Wes Bentley, Mena Suvari, Peter Gallagher, Allison Janney

DIRECTOR ....Sam Mendes

WRITER...Alan Ball

There's nothing like a movie about a man's mid-life crisis to remind us that finding ourselves is something that we're going to have to do more than once in our lives, whenever we're breaking out of our comfort zones.

There is bound to come a time for all of us when we have to take a look at our lives and realize that we'd rather be working at Happy Burger than going to that dead-end job for one more day, and that we really do need to spring for that sports car and the DVD player WITH shuffle capacity, and tool around town blasting show tunes until we figure out what to do with our lives.

And that is exactly what Lester Burnham (Kevin Spacey) does when he discovers in the middle of his life that he hasn't really lived at all. He is stuck in a job that isn't right for him, working for people who don't respect him, to support a family that doesn't understand him, and maintain a lifestyle that doesn't make him happy.

And so Lester, driven to desperate measures by the closet of quiet desperation, breaks down and does the unthinkable: He starts to do crunches. And before you know it he's whaling on his pecs, blasting personal empowerment anthems, smoking pot, spending money foolishly, and talking back to his superiors. Beneath the surface of what looks like a completely predictable mid-life crisis, a wonderful transformation is beginning, and soon a butterfly of a whole new color begins to emerge from the chrysalis of Lester's middle-age slump.

So if you're feeling trapped in a job description that just doesn't match your skills, watch *American Beauty* and let Lester's personal revolution inspire you to stand up and reinvent yourself, then tell the world who you really are, not because they'll listen, but because you will.

KEVIN'S CRUMPETS

"I feel like I've been in a coma for the past twenty years.
And I'm just now waking up."

. . . .

"I want to look good naked!"

. . . .

"Janie, today I quit my job. And then I told my boss
to go fuck himself, and then I blackmailed him
for almost sixty thousand dollars. Pass the asparagus."

. . . .

"I guess I could be pretty pissed off about what happened to me,
but it's hard to be angry when there's so much beauty in the world.
Sometimes, I feel like I'm seeing it all at once, and I can't take it.
My heart swells up like a balloon that's about to burst.
But then I remember to relax, and stop trying to hold on to it.
And then, it flows through me like rain and I feel nothing
but gratitude for every single moment of my stupid little life."

KEVIN SPACEY

AS LESTER BURNHAM IN *AMERICAN BEAUTY*

SHOWGIRLS (1995)

STARS . . . . Elizabeth Berkley, Kyle MacLachlan, Gina Gershon

DIRECTOR . . . . Paul Verhoeven

WRITER . . . . Joe Eszterhas

Is someone throwing beads under your toe shoes during your big number? Watch *Showgirls* and let this story about a small-town girl who makes it big in the burlesque show of life remind you that all that glitters is not necessarily Versace.

Nomi Malone (Elizabeth Berkley) is a girl with a checkered past who moves to Las Vegas in search of fame and fortune. She quickly finds a friend in Molly Abrams (Gina Ravera) and a job stripping at the Chita. After an extremely aggressive pole dance and some backroom time with the "Goddess" director and star, Nomi lands a job as a chorus girl and the interest of star Cristal Connors (Gina Gershon), who decides she wants Nomi to do her nails. But Nomi has a few nails of her own, and in no time she's pushed Cristal back into the gem polisher, and it's Nomi who is the one exploding naked out of a smoldering volcano, and learning that the costs of losing touch with your authentic self in search of fame and fortune include an over-inflated production budget, wooden dialogue, and disappointment at the box office.

PEARLS FROM PORNOGRAPHERS

"It must be weird, not having anybody cum on you."

ROBERT DAVI

AS AL TORRES IN *SHOWGIRLS*

"Okay, ladies, I'm Tony Moss. I produce this show.
Some of you have probably heard that I'm a prick. I am a prick.
I got one interest here, and that's the show. I don't care
whether you live or die. I want to see you dance and
I want to see you smile. I can't use you if you can't smile,
I can't use you if you can't show, I can't use you if you can't sell."

ALAN RACHINS

AS TONY MOSS IN *SHOWGIRLS*

Nomi: "I'm not a whore, I'm a dancer!"
Cristal: "We're all whores darlin'. We take the cash,
we cash the check, we show them what they want to see."

ELIZABETH BERKLEY AND GINA GERSHON

AS NOMI MALONE AND CRISTAL CONNORS IN *SHOWGIRLS*

VALLEY OF THE DOLLS (1967)

STARS ....Barbara Parkins, Patty Duke, Sharon Tate,
..........................Susan Hayward, Lee Grant, Paul Burke, Tony Scotti

DIRECTOR..Mark Robson

WRITERS ....Helen Deutsch, Dorothy Kingsley,
..................................based on the novel by Jacqueline Susann

When you're feeling a little winded by your climb up to the heights of success and you've gotta get off, gotta get off the merry-go-round, let Neely (Patty Duke) and Anne (Barbara Parkins) and Jennifer (Sharon Tate) remind you that the secret to managing the peaks and valleys of life is to never lose track of yourself and where you come from.

Valley of the Dolls, which was the *Showgirls* of its day, is the screen adaptation of Jacqueline Susann's pulp novel of the same name, in which three young bright-eyed and bushy-tailed would-be starlets arrive in the Big Apple in search of fame and fortune. And they find it—as well as power, corruption, greed, a couple of casting couches, and a lot of refillable prescriptions for mood enhancers, which they pop into their mouths like salted peanuts between belts of bourbon.

Sound like your kind of party? Well just wait and see what happens to these beautiful creatures once they lose track of the one thing that you need when you're teetering on the cliff far above the valley: the confidence to stand on your own two feet and a shoulder to lean on that doesn't require prescriptions in triplicate.

REALITY CHECK

Judy Garland, upon whom many have said the Neely O'Hara character in *Valley of the Dolls* was based, was originally cast in the role of Helen Lawson. Judy demanded, and received, a pool table in her dressing room, but not even a good game of billiards could keep Judy in the film, and she eventually backed out and was replaced by Susan Hayward. When she walked off the set, Judy kept the now-famous sequin pantsuit, which she wore in her comeback at Carnegie Hall.

VALLEY GIRLS

**"The only hit that comes out of a Helen Lawson production
is Helen Lawson, and that's ME, baby, remember?"**

. . . .

"Broadway doesn't go for booze and dope."

SUSAN HAYWARD

AS HELEN LAWSON IN *VALLEY OF THE DOLLS*

**"Take these papers to Helen Lawson and don't give her any of that
'I loved you when I was a child' crap or she'll stab you in the back."**

ROBERT HARRIS

AS HENRY BELLAMY IN *VALLEY OF THE DOLLS*

**"I have to get up at five o'clock in the morning
and SPARKLE, Neely, SPARKLE!"**

PATTY DUKE

AS NEELY O'HARA IN *VALLEY OF THE DOLLS*

"You've got to climb Mount Everest to reach the Valley of the Dolls."

BARBARA PARKINS

AS ANNE WELLES IN *VALLEY OF THE DOLLS*

JENNY JONES "MAKEOVER" MOVIES

So your pants are fitting a little more tightly and you have to breathe in to get the top button done, and when you look in the mirror you think you've seen better heads on a johnny mop. Get down off your cross because someone needs the wood and watch one of these Jenny Jones "makeover" movies because when you know how fabulous you are, it's easy for others to see it too.

HAIRSPRAY (1988)

STARS...........................Ricki Lake, Sonny Bono, Ruth Brown, Divine,
....Deborah Harry, Colleen Fitzpatrick

DIRECTOR ....John Waters

WRITER ....John Waters

Tracy Turnblad (Ricki Lake) is a hair hopper. She is round and isn't afraid to shake it, baby, shake it. Unfortunately, those around her think big girls should be out of sight and out of mind. They also feel this way about African-Americans and I'm sure anyone else who is different from them. But Tracy rises above it all and presses on more than just a set of Lee Nails to make her dreams come true.

Armed with her talent and self-confidence (not to mention huge-ass hair and one-of-a-kind dresses), Tracy dances her way to stardom and integration, and reminds all of us hair hoppers that the best makeovers work from the inside out.

DEATH BECOMES HER (1992)

STARS . . . . Meryl Streep, Bruce Willis, Goldie Hawn, Isabella Rossellini

DIRECTOR . . . . Robert Zemeckis

WRITERS . . . . Martin Donovan, David Koepp

We all strive for physical perfection and timeless beauty, but as this movie shows us, you better be careful what you wish for because you might get it.

Madeline Ashton (Meryl Streep) and Helen Sharp (Goldie Hawn) discover that they're sharing the same man. After Helen realizes she's lost the race, a nervous breakdown ensues. It's not long before she's swinging again with a new best-selling book under her belt, as well as a new hot little figure, and steals Ernest (Bruce Willis) back. Then Helen and Madeline realize that they have more than a man and plastic surgeon in common: They also share the burden of eternal life and beauty. It's at Ernest's funeral that we see what kind of "gift" it really is, and we, along with our heroines, learn that perfection and eternity are nothing compared to being organically connected to the natural flow of life and that nothing that is truly beautiful is ever perfect.

SHREK (2001)

STARS . . . . Mike Myers, Eddie Murphy, Cameron Diaz, John Lithgow

DIRECTORS . . . . Andrew Adamson, Vicky Jenson

WRITERS . . . . William Steig, Ted Elliott,
. . . . Terry Rossio, Joe Stillman, Roger S.H. Schulman

Shrek (Mike Myers) is a big, smelly, green ogre who lives in the woods. Years of being different have made him bitter and jaded, and he's basically shut the world out, posted No Trespassing signs all over his emotional swamp, and slammed the door on society.

Enter a loudmouth donkey (Eddie Murphy), an overtly articulate Princess Fiona (Cameron Diaz), and Lord Farquaad of Duloc (John Lithgow as the bad guy), who is holding Shrek's swamp ransom. Princess Fiona is in need of a kiss so she can be transformed into love's true form. Shrek just wants his house back, and the donkey just needs some excitement and friends. So begins the adventure.

When Princess Fiona finally gets her kiss, everyone is surprised by the makeover that true love brings about in the beauty and the beast. When you're stuck in a search for love's true form, let Shrek remind you that fairy tales can come true, they can happen to you.

I'M THE ONE THAT I WANT (2000)

STARS...Margaret Cho

DIRECTOR..Lionel Coleman

WRITER...Margaret Cho

If you're feeling miscast in the sitcom of your life, let Margaret Cho's liberating journey from self-loathing to self-love inspire you to demand control, no matter what the creative consultants in your life may think about it.

In this movie version of her show at San Francisco's Warfield Theatre in 1999, Margaret tells the story of her first shot at the big time: a TV show based on her life called *The All-American Girl.* From the moment the Gods of Hollywood mutter those magical words, "Margaret, Margaret Cho, you're going to be a STAR!" Margaret feels accepted. She feels appreciated. She feels validated. And she feels really, really hungry.

As soon as the cameras start rolling, the network tries to change everything that makes Margaret Margaret. They tell her to lose thirty pounds because her face is too big. They hire an American "Asian consultant" to teach Margaret how to be more Asian-American, put her on an exercise regimen that would trim a small nation, and, worst of all, demand that she stop telling jokes about her mother. When all efforts fail to change her into a network version of herself, the bubble bursts, as bubbles made out of hot air and soap are inclined to do, and the Gods of Hollywood cancel her show.

In the end, Margaret must learn that the only kind of acceptance that really matters is the kind that comes from appreciating your own unique voice and your own unique shape, and being free to satisfy your own unique appetites.

WIZARD OF OZ (1939)

STARS .... Judy Garland, Frank Morgan, Ray Bolger, Bert Lahr,
.... Jack Haley, Billie Burke, Margaret Hamilton

DIRECTORS .... Victor Fleming, Richard Thorpe, King Vidor

WRITERS .... Noel Langley, Florence Ryerson, Edgar Allan Woolf,
.... based on the novel *The Wonderful Wizard of Oz* by L. Frank Baum

You know, you're not the first little girl from Kansas to dream of flying off to a place where there isn't any trouble—a place you can't get to by boat or train because it's far, far away, behind the moon, beyond the rain . . . you get the idea.

It's a familiar tale to all of us by now. Dorothy (Judy Garland), a young and impressionable girl from the great monochromatic fly-over, dreams of a technicolor world far away from the hog farms of home. One day deliverance arrives in the form of a natural disaster. It wipes out the neighborhood and transports Dorothy to a rainbow world, where she is free to express her edgy sense of color for the very first time but is also completely guilt-conflicted about wiping out her entire community, not to mention the witch she squashes upon landing in order to achieve her creative independence.

So what does Dorothy do now that she, after great personal expense, at last finds herself in the land of her dreams, populated with good witches and wicked witches, flying monkeys and lollipop gangs, and sweeping fields of poppies? Well, she does what a lot of us would do; she picks up one guy who can't think (Ray Bolger), another guy who can't love (Jack Haley), and another guy who can't stand up for himself (Bert Lahr). Together they go in search of a man who will take charge—a big daddy behind the curtain (Frank Morgan) who will solve all their problems and send Dorothy back to the very same hog farm she just fought so hard to escape.

We friends of Dorothy who remain in Oz wonder what might have happened if Dorothy had taken in a few of the sights, eaten in a few local restaurants, or danced with the Lollipop Guild. She might have discovered a whole new world and a whole new family beyond her backyard. She might have realized that the one place where there isn't any trouble is the quiet spot inside yourself where you are self-confident enough to find happiness wherever the wind might drop you.

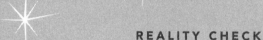

REALITY CHECK

There is a whole universe of urban legend that has grown up around Dorothy Gale's technicolor weekend spree in the land of Oz. Here are a few of our favorites, which we're pretty sure are true. But if you have any doubts, go see the wizard.

* The Munchkins on the set were paid $50 per week for a six-day work week, which is less than half of what Toto was paid.

* At the beginning of the "We're Off to See the Wizard" number, many swear they can see a Munchkin hanging himself. People in the know, however, insist it is a large bird stretching its wings. Watch and see what you think.

* Originally, Dorothy wore a blonde wig and heavy makeup, and looked a lot like the Swiss Miss girl on hallucinogens. When Victor Fleming took over direction of the picture, though, he got rid of the wig and the makeup and told Judy just to be herself.

* In 1970, Liza Minnelli married Jack Haley, Jr., who is the son of Jack Haley, Sr., who played the Tin Man.

* Dorothy was the main inspiration for the character of Mary Ann on *Gilligan's Island*.

WORDS FROM THE WISE?

"Now you go feed those hogs before they worry themselves into anemia!"

CLARA BLANDICK
AS AUNTIE EM IN *THE WIZARD OF OZ*

"Professor Marvel never guesses. He knows!"

FRANK MORGAN
AS PROFESSOR MARVEL IN *THE WIZARD OF OZ*

"Pay no attention to that man behind the curtain."

. . . .

"A heart is not judged by how much you love, but by how much you are loved by others."

FRANK MORGAN
AS THE WIZARD OF OZ IN *THE WIZARD OF OZ*

"Oh, Auntie Em—there's no place like home!"

JUDY GARLAND
AS DOROTHY IN *THE WIZARD OF OZ*

CHAPTER TEN

THE NEW HAPPILY EVER AFTER

We-Are-Family Movies

Let's all just admit it and get over it already: We're not living in a "he and she and baby makes three" world anymore. Families come in as many different shapes, sizes, and geometric configurations as people do, and it's time we acknowledged that family happens wherever there are friends, co-workers, cats, dogs, goldfish, and yes, even blood relations, who love and support one another.

So if you're wondering if there's a happily ever after that includes the rest of us, or if you're just in the mood to get together with the people that matter most and count your blessings, watch one of these We-Are-Family movies about connections of the soul, and celebrate the fact that these days, you actually can pick your relatives!

HAROLD AND MAUDE (1971)

STARS...Bud Cort, Ruth Gordon

DIRECTOR...Hal Ashby

WRITER ....Colin Higgins I

Never was there a more unlikely but beautiful family of the soul than Harold and Maude. Harold is a poor little rich boy with an absent father, a domineering mother, a fascination with death, funerals, and staging his own suicide, and who seems, given all of the above, like the only thing he's really dying to do is come out of the closet.

Then there's Maude (Ruth Gordon), a seventy-nine-year-old Holocaust survivor who has the energy and joie de vivre of a flower child in the August of her summer of love.

And while one normally encounters muses of this genre in neighborhood piano bars after one too many Whiskey Sours and Barbra Streisand ballads, Harold first meets his Maude at the funeral of a person that neither one of them knows. Their paths cross when Ruth steals Harold's souped-up hearse, Harold jumps into the passenger seat, and together they hit the road. While what they discover is not always an easy answer, they do learn, right along with us, that family means someone who sees your inner light and helps you to let it shine.

MAUDE'S MORSELS

"A lot of people enjoy being dead. But they're not dead, really.
They're just . . . backing away from life. Reach out. Take a chance.
Get hurt, even! Play as well as you can. Go team! GO! Give me an L!
Give me an I! Give me a V! Give me an E! L-I-V-E. LIVE!
Otherwise, you got nothing to talk about in the locker room."

. . . .

"You see, Harold, I feel that much of the world's sorrow comes from
people who are 'this,' yet allow themselves to be treated as 'that.'"

. . . .

"Vice, virtue, it's best not to be too moral—
you cheat yourself out of too much life. Aim above morality."

RUTH GORDON
AS MAUDE IN *HAROLD AND MAUDE*

STEEL MAGNOLIAS (1989)

STARS . . . . Sally Field, Dolly Parton, Shirley MacLaine,
. . . . Olympia Dukakis, Julia Roberts, Daryl Hannah,
. . . . Sam Shepard, Dylan McDermott

DIRECTOR . . . . Herbert Ross

WRITER . . . . Robert Harling, based on the play by Robert Harling

If you're in the mood for a night in with just you and the family, indulge in a little emotional wash and tease with *Steel Magnolias,* and let Miss Truvy's beauty-parlor family put the poof back in your bouff.

This story threads through the seasons of a small southern parish: Growing up and moving on; holding tight and letting go; life, death, and life in a small town where your neighbors are your extended family . . . basically all that stuff that either drives you to drink or builds character, or both. We meet this family of southern belles at Truvy's Hair Salon on the wedding day of Shelby Eatenton (Julia Roberts), the prettiest girl in town, who is marrying the prettiest boy (Dylan McDermott), in a haze of Pepto Bismol pink and good southern small-town family feeling. After a diabetic attack, lots of hair teasing, a few untimely deaths, and even more gossip, we start to realize that just as walls have ears, every hairdo has a story. We also remember, along with all of the women at the beauty salon, that there isn't a bad hair day that can't be overcome so long as you've got friends to tuck in your split ends.

BEAUTY-PARLOR PUNDITS

"In a good shoe, I wear a size six,
but a seven feels so good, I buy a size eight."

DOLLY PARTON
AS TRUVY IN *STEEL MAGNOLIAS*

"I do not see plays, because I can nap at home for free.
And I don't see movies 'cause they're trash, and they got nothin'
but naked people in 'em! And I don't read books, 'cause if they're
any good, they're gonna make 'em into a miniseries."

SHIRLEY MACLAINE
AS OUISER IN *STEEL MAGNOLIAS*

"Miss Truvy, I promise that my personal tragedy
will not interfere with my ability to do good hair."

DARYL HANNAH
AS ANNELLE IN *STEEL MAGNOLIAS*

"All gay men have track lightin'.
And all gay men are named Mark, Rick, or Steve."

· ·

"The only thing that separates us from the animals
is our ability to accessorize."

OLYMPIA DUKAKIS
AS CLAIREE IN *STEEL MAGNOLIAS*

BILLY ELLIOT (2000)

STARS.................Jamie Bell, Julie Walters, Gary Lewis, Jamie Draven,
....Mike Elliot, Nicola Blackwell

DIRECTOR ....Stephen Daldry

WRITER ....Lee Hall

As one who was trapped in a small town with pirouettes in my heart and basketball and track shoes on my feet, I consider *Billy Elliot* one of my favorite movies by far. How does one break down stereotypes, disappoint loved ones, face embarrassment, and deal with financial issues just to follow a dream, to dance?

Billy Elliot (Jamie Bell) is an eleven-year-old boy with a family hit hard by the economics of 1984 northern England, which only adds to his adolescent struggle. Although his family is close, his mother has died, his brother and father are focused on a work strike, and Billy is forced to take care of his ailing grandmother. Soon, he finds a hidden talent and passion, dancing.

When dad (Gary Lewis) finds out about Billy's ballet secret, he quickly pulls him out of his ballet slippers and his dream. With the help of his teacher (Julie Walters), who sees his talents, Billy and "Miss" secretly work day and night to land him a scholarship at a nearby dance school. When dad finally gets to see Billy dance, he knows he must let go of his issues and let his son live out what he was meant to do.

So, when you're longing to dance but stuck in the boxing ring of your life, find the strength to grand jeté over that high hurdle. You may find not only a hidden talent but the happiness you've been longing for.

CELL MATES

THE CRYING GAME (1992)

STARS ...... Forest Whitaker, Stephen Rea, Miranda Richardson, Jaye Davidson

DIRECTOR .... Neil Jordan

WRITER .... Neil Jordan

Fergus (Stephen Rea), a soldier in the IRA, is assigned to guard Jody (Forest Whitaker), a British soldier who has been taken captive for the cause. Jody and Fergus talk all through the night and, surprisingly, begin to love each other, either due to the Stockholm Syndrome or the resilient quality of love that can bloom like a rose even in the cement of Irish–British politics.

Later, haunted by the memory of that love and concern for this man who has somehow become a brother of the soul, Fergus goes to London in search of Jody's girlfriend, Dil, and finds her singing "The Crying Game" in a low-rent honky-tonk on the wrong side of town; he falls instantly in love. Unbeknownst to Fergus, however, is that Dil isn't your average run-of-the-mill torch diva. She is an enigmatic boundary bleeder, who not only crosses gender lines but also the seemingly unbridgeable chasm between Britain and the IRA.

The love that grows between all of the unlikely soul mates in this story reminds us that whether we are in a soldier's uniform or a slinky cocktail dress, we are all members of the same human family who can find a way to live in peace, if we come from a place of love and understanding.

SILENCE OF THE LAMBS (1991)

STARS ....Jodie Foster, Anthony Hopkins, Scott Glenn, Ted Levine

DIRECTOR...Jonathan Demme

WRITERS ....Ted Tally, Thomas Harris (novel)

The bond that forms between FBI agent Clarisse Starling (Jodie Foster) and serial killer Hannibal Lecter (Anthony Hopkins) is one of the more intriguing ever drawn, and is also a chilling reminder about what can happen when you reenact absent-father issues in the workplace. Clarisse must unlock the secrets of this psychiatrist-turned-serial-killer's elegant but lethal soul, but in exchange, she must reveal her own. Is this a cat-and-mouse game between an interrogator and her prisoner or the twisted dance of two soul mates struggling to reach through the bars and find a person they can belong to? Clarisse and her cannibal suggest that the soul has a few appetites that are best not satisfied.

THE INTERVIEW (1998)

STARS ....Hugo Weaving, Tony Martin

DIRECTOR...Craig Monahan

WRITERS...................................Craig Monahan, Gordon Davie

The police raid mild-mannered, average-Aussie-guy Eddie's (Hugo Weaving's) home in the middle of the night while he's asleep in his bed. He's taken at gunpoint to an interrogation room and left to sweat and wonder at this strange turn of events.

At last, Detective John Steele (Tony Martin), his interrogator, arrives, and what ensues is an intricate chess match between two souls who must look to each other for redemption and leave us all wondering who is guilty and who is innocent. This movie reminds us that family consists of the people who are willing to go out on a limb and tell us things that we may not want to hear.

ABSOLUTELY FABULOUS (1992)

STARS . . . . Jennifer Saunders, Joanna Lumley, Julia Sawalha

DIRECTOR . . . . Bob Spiers

WRITERS . . . . Jennifer Saunders,
. . . . based on an idea by Jennifer Saunders and Dawn French

When you're feeling bogged down by the trivial details of life—like men, emotional maturity, your job, or your mother—then throw an impromptu Ab-Fabathon with your family of the heart, and hitch a ride on a champagne bubble up, up, and away from the daily grind.

Patsy (Joanna Lumley) and Edina (Jennifer Saunders) are two absolutely fabulous friends who break just about every rule in life's little instruction book. They don't floss or say please and thank you. They put nothing by for a rainy day and rarely turn their frowns upside down. They choose style over substance, quantity over quality, they ignore the Golden Rule because it doesn't have a designer label, they never do anything in moderation, and they never, but never, give Eddy's priggish daughter, Saffy (Julia Sawalha), the time of day.

Yet somehow, despite some of the most wickedly hilarious and appallingly bad relationship skills to ever stagger and slur their way into our living rooms, Patsy and Edina—and even Saffy—understand what's truly important in life: lunch, champagne, shopping, and each other, although they may not always agree on the order.

So the next time you're in the mood to climb back into the nest, kick back and regress with your own sweetie darlings, and remember that while we may trip over the hemline of life from time to time, and in a pair of truly atrocious pumps, we might add, there is still nothing quite as absolutely fabulous as a family of friends and relations that you can count on.

EDINA'S EGG FLIPS

"I want total sensory deprivation and backup drugs!"

. . . .

"It's called colonic irrigation, dahling. It's not to be sniffed at."

JENNIFER SAUNDERS

AS EDINA IN "ABSOLUTELY FABULOUS"

. . . .

PATSY'S PUNCH

"Darling, you are a fabulous, wonderful individual, and remember, I've known you longer than your daughter has! Eddy, can I take the car?"

. . . .

**"I thought a little mosey down Bond Street,
a little sniff around Gucci, sidle up to Ralph Lauren,
pass through Browns and on to Quags for a light lunch."**

. . . .

"The last mosquito that bit me had to book into the Betty Ford Clinic."

JOANNA LUMLEY

AS PATSY IN "ABSOLUTELY FABULOUS"

SHE WORKS HARD FOR IT, HONEY

When you've both had a tough day at the office, punch out with one of these working-girl heroes, then curl up with your office family after hours, and remember that Domino's Pizza delivers.

NINE TO FIVE (1980)

STARS ....Jane Fonda, Lily Tomlin, Dolly Parton, Dabney Coleman

DIRECTOR ....Colin Higgins

WRITERS.............Patricia Resnick, Colin Higgins, story by Patricia Resnick

If you've had a rough day in the steno pool and you're in the mood to teach that sexist, egotistical, lying hypocritical bigot a lesson he'll never forget, let Judy (Jane Fonda), Doralee (Dolly Parton), and Violet (Lily Tomlin), three secretaries who get even, help you vent a little of that pent-up angst, without having to hit the unemployment line in the morning.

CLOCKWATCHERS (1997)

STARS.................Toni Collette, Parker Posey, Lisa Kudrow, Alanna Ubach

DIRECTOR ....Jill Sprecher

WRITERS.......................................Jill Sprecher, Karen Sprecher

When you're feeling like a temp in the multinational conglomerate of life, join forces with the corporate orphans of Global Credit, and let these working-girl heroes with dreams that are bigger than their job descriptions remind you that you're as successful as you think you are, as long as you don't compromise yourself.

WORKING GIRL (1988)

STARS . . . . Melanie Griffith, Sigourney Weaver, Harrison Ford

DIRECTOR . . . . Mike Nichols

WRITER . . . . Kevin Wade

Are you fed up with doing all of the work and getting none of the rewards? Has your boss been stealing your thunder? Strike back with Tess McGill (Melanie Griffith), who takes on the powers that be and winds up getting the raise, the corner office, the designer stockings, AND Harrison Ford, and all because when opportunity knocks, Tess isn't afraid to bust down the door.

POST-ITS FROM THE STENO POOL

"I'm no fool. I've killed the boss;
you think they're not gonna fire me for a thing like that?!"

LILY TOMLIN
AS VIOLET IN *NINE TO FIVE*

"You can't fire me! You don't even know my NAME!"

PARKER POSEY
AS MARGARET IN *CLOCKWATCHERS*

"I have a head for business and a bod for sin.
Is there anything wrong with that?"

. . . .

"I am not steak. You can't just order me."

MELANIE GRIFFITH
AS TESS IN *WORKING GIRL*

THE BIRDCAGE (1996)

STARS .... Calista Flockhart, Dan Futterman, Gene Hackman, ... Nathan Lane, Dianne Wiest, Robin Williams

DIRECTOR .... Mike Nichols

WRITER ...... Elaine May, based on the play *La Cage aux Folles* by Jean Poiret

Have you ever been embarrassed by your strange and unusual family? All families, in their own ways, seem strange to their children, but when Mom is a drag queen and Dad runs the nightclub she performs in, it can make things a li'l weird.

When Val Goldman (Dan Futterman) decides to get married, bringing his intended's parents (Gene Hackman and Dianne Wiest) home to meet his parents will prove to be a problem. For one, his future father-in-law is a very conservative senator. Secondly, Val has two Daddies. So he's forced to ask Dad and Dad (Robin Williams and Nathan Lane) to pretend to be totally different from what they are, not to mention change their house and get rid of Nathan Lane. When the in-laws show up, as well as Nathan Lane's Albert, things get interesting.

So, when you're feeling the need to change literally everything about yourself or your family to fit into someone else's mold, watch *The Birdcage* and celebrate the gift of being eccentric.

QUESTIONS WE DON'T WANT ANSWERED

Agador: "When you gonna let me audition for your show?"
Armand: "When you have talent."

HANK AZARIA AND ROBIN WILLIAMS
AS AGADOR AND ARMAND IN *THE BIRDCAGE*

THE YEAR OF LIVING
DANGEROUSLY (1982)

STARS . . . . Mel Gibson, Sigourney Weaver, Linda Hunt

DIRECTOR . . . . Peter Weir

WRITERS . . . . . . Peter Weir, David Williamson, based on the novel by C. J. Koch

It is often said that if you want to know the world, love one another. And such is the case with fledgling but ambitious Aussie reporter Guy Hamilton (Mel Gibson), who goes to Jakarta in 1965, the final year of Sukarno's communist regime. Once there, he finds himself locked out of the colonial old-boys' network of reporters who treat this capital of the Third World like an English gentlemen's club and are oblivious to the cultural and human implications of the news that they are covering. But Guy isn't like that, there's something sensitive about him, and not just because of those azure-as-an-Aspen-sky-in-September eyes, either. Guy has a vulnerability that is immediately recognized by Billy Kwan (Linda Hunt, in an Oscar-winning drag performance), a native photojournalist who feels deeply for the plight of his people and who chooses Guy to tell the truth about the suffering in Jakarta.

And so Billy leads Guy on a personally guided tour through the highs and lows of Indonesian culture, knitting a web of understanding and compassion between the Western and the developing world, and in some small way, healing both cultures through the love and understanding that is forged between these two unlikely soul mates, brought together under the curse of interesting times.

This movie is a great reminder that soul mates come in all shapes, colors, and sizes, and that when we come to love and understand someone who is very different from us we not only enrich our own lives, but in our own small way do our part toward creating a more tolerant and loving world.

ALL YOU NEED IS LOVE

"We'll make a great team, old man.
You for the words, me for the pictures. I can be your eyes."

LINDA HUNT
AS BILLY KWAN IN *THE YEAR OF LIVING DANGEROUSLY*

"But I always think that the best way to
know God is to love many things."

VINCENT VAN GOGH

MY OWN PRIVATE IDAHO (1991)

STARS . . . . River Phoenix, Keanu Reeves, James Russo

DIRECTOR . . . . Gus Van Sant

WRITER . . . . Gus Van Sant

If you've been searching the world over for a place that feels like home and people who feel like family, but so far every exit ramp turns into a jug handle on the Garden State Parkway of Life, let Gus Van Sant's spiritual street hustler remind you that the security of a home and a family starts with feeling secure inside yourself, and being awake to the opportunities for love right in front of you.

Mike Waters (River Phoenix) is a narcoleptic teenage hustler in Portland, Oregon, who is a self-dubbed connoisseur of roads, mostly because he spends his life passing out in the middle of them. Fortunately, Mike's best friend, Scott Favor (Keanu Reeves), is there to scrape him off the asphalt. Scott is the scion of a wealthy family who is called to a life of privilege but chooses instead to turn tricks for a living, mostly because it pisses off his father.

For a time, these two boys find a home in each other. As things often happen, though, in a Gus Van Sant allegory with many Shakespearean allusions, a love triangle emerges when Mike falls in love with Scott, and Scott falls in love with some beautiful Italian chick that he meets while he's moonlighting on the right side of town.

Will Scott resume his life as the favored son of an aging metaphor for conformity and capitalist greed? Or will he be there to peel River Phoenix off the asphalt? Or will he find a way to make a family that includes everyone he loves? We're not going to let you in on the answer to that question; however, we will tell you that when you're wandering the world over in search of a road home, make sure to look both ways before you cross the street.

CHAPTER TEN: THE NEW HAPPILY EVER AFTER: WE-ARE-FAMILY MOVIES

207

THE RULES OF THE ROAD

"I'm a connoisseur of roads. I've been tasting roads my whole life.
This road will never end. It probably goes all around the world."

RIVER PHOENIX

AS MIKE WATERS IN *MY OWN PRIVATE IDAHO*

"When you wake up, wipe the slugs off your face.
Be ready for a new day!"

· ·

"When I left home, the maid asked me where I was off to.
I said 'Wherever. Whatever. Have a nice day.' "

· ·

"It's when you start doing things for free
that you start to grow wings."

KEANU REEVES

AS SCOTT FAVOR IN *MY OWN PRIVATE IDAHO*

"It doesn't matter what you do in the bedroom as long as you don't
do it in the street and frighten the horses."

DAPHNE FIELDING

THE DUCHESS OF JERMYN STREET

"What is straight? A line can be straight or a street, but the human
heart, oh, no, it's curved like a road through mountains."

TENNESSEE WILLIAMS

A STREETCAR NAMED DESIRE

A

B

C

D

E

F

G

S

ABOUT THE AUTHORS

Beverly West (co-author of the best-selling *Cinematherapy* series) and Jason Bergund (dancer, choreographer, and obsessed movie fan) are best friends and co-pug parents living together on the Upper West Side of Manhattan.